# The Inside Game
## to Real Estate Value Investing

*Winning Strategies and Opportunities
for Value Oriented Real Estate Investors!*

By
**Craig Haskell**

Publisher:

Haskell Value Investor LLC
23005 N. 15th Ave
Suite 201
Phoenix, AZ 85027
623-582-9766

This publication is intended to provide accurate and authoritative information with regard to the subject matter covered. It is offered with the understanding that neither the publisher nor the author is engaged in rendering legal, tax or other professional advice or services. If legal, tax or other expert assistance is needed, the services of a competent professional should be sought.

This book is intended for instructional purposes only. Readers are advised to proceed with the techniques described herein with caution. Neither the author nor publisher makes any warranties, expressed or implied, about the merchantability or fitness for any particular use of this product.

ISBN 978-1-257-02108-6

# Table of Contents

## PART 1

# PART 2

# Introduction

*"Now is the time to lay our foundation for value creation. Now is the time to pick our spots. Now is the time to rummage through the distress in the marketplace and find opportunities. Now is the time, my fellow value investors, to put on our Value Hound suits and get in the game."*

Craig Haskell, Value Hound
Haskell Value Real Estate Investor

Many investors are playing the value investing game on *Wall Street*, buying and selling stocks and bonds. Investors buy undervalued stocks and then later resell them for a profit. If an investor wants to learn the ins and outs of value investing in the stock space, there are tons of books, radios shows, TV shows, seminars, conferences and published information on how to use value investing strategies to make money in the stock market. Do a search on Google using the term "value investing" and pages and pages of returns show up for the term, value investing. Many professionals have dissected and uncovered the details of value investing in the stock market to benefit knowledge seeking investors.

The value investing game is also played in the field of real estate. Billions upon billions of dollars are invested every year in the real estate value investing space. There are many real estate value investors around the world executing various value strategies. A lot of money has been made in the real estate value arena from small investors buying a single family house to large investors buying a $100 million commercial real estate property.

However, very little has been written on the process and strategies of real estate value investing. Do the same Google search for the term "real estate value investing" and only a few returns show up. Search around and you will find very little information available to new and experienced investors on what's working and not working in the real estate value investing space. There is great value in learning new ideas and strategies for real estate investors to become more successful with their real estate investments.

We need to do better as an industry to educate, inform and train on the principles of real estate value investing. We can reach new heights by expanding the pie and creating an environment of new possibilities and opportunities to exceed best practices. In that pursuit, we can become stronger and more active leaders to advance better ways of doing things, creating more opportunities for all connected to this specialized space.

In an attempt to provide a much needed resource and leadership to our industry, I created a new on-line publication dedicated exclusively to opportunistic and value minded real estate investors called the *Haskell Value Real Estate Investor*. The mission is to empower our community of investors, executives and entrepreneurs to change the status quo, learn new ideas and strategies, connect with more committed like-minded people and find more profitable opportunities within our specialized niche. To get more information, check out the website at www.HaskellValueRealEstateInvestor.com

It has become my challenge to become the world's leading resource for opportunistic and value real estate investors. I have created a growing interview series with the industry's brightest minds and innovators. These interviews offer exclusive insight from the world's leading value investors, financiers, entrepreneurs and top executives.

From these interviews, you'll get an inside look at unique opportunistic and value real estate investing strategies. Here are the types of value strategies you will learn more about:

- How to buy distressed low priced real estate at well below replacement cost
- How to buy distressed troubled loans and notes
- How to buy under-performing income property and raise rents
- How to convert a property to another higher and better use
- How to build and add additional square footage to existing property

- How to buy in rebounding high growth national markets
- How to buy lower class properties and reposition to higher class properties
- How to buy a property and reposition to target niche tenant base

It is my mission to hunt down and uncover new strategies, deals, money investors, opportunities and critical service providers that are active in the real estate value investing space so that investors have the very best information to make smarter decisions.

Inside this book, you will find a condensed version of interviews that I've done with some of today's leading real estate value investors. Find out what they are doing. What sets them apart? Why have they been so successful? What strategies are they employing to build their portfolios?

**Inside The Game**

This book will help you learn new ideas to take advantage of today's value real estate investing opportunities so that you can achieve financial independence. Whether you are a new or experienced investor, this book uncovers the inside game of value real estate investing and the strategies you can use to create value and make more money with your real estate investments.

I have written this book to expose the inside game of value real estate investing for investors seeking specialized information. This book goes into detail on the principles, the strategies and the process of real estate value investing.

In the first part of the book, I delve into the foundation of real estate value investing. What is real estate value investing? What is the framework and methodology behind real estate value investing? How does an investor use the value investing framework? What strategies are real estate value investors using today? Why should you become a real estate value investor? What are the results of being a real estate value investor? Why today is the best time in a lifetime to be a real estate value investor? You will understand real estate value investing and how to use it to improve your investment performance.

You will read an interview with Jerome Fink on how he became one of the top real estate value investors in the country buying and repositioning multifamily properties. His initial goal, when he started his company in 1996, was to buy only 500 units. Learn how he managed to buy and sell over 52,000 units and do 200 property renovations.

In the second part of the book, I give you a complete process of real estate value investing so that you know where to begin, when to do it, why to do it, and most importantly, how to do it. You will learn:

- How to find great value creation opportunities like a true Value Hound
- How to analyze a deal so that you know you have a winner
- How to find partners to fund your value deals
- How to structure an investment with partners and investors
- How to hire a top notch property management company
- How to execute a value creation strategy to lock in profits
- How to create a support network to help you through the process
- How to use the Value Hound blueprint so that you can invest full-time.

In the last chapter, I give you a step-by-step process to follow to build your own investment syndication business using real estate value investing strategies. You will find a very conservative sample syndication model plan that shows how you can achieve financial freedom in three years.

Learn how "Rance" King of RK Properties over the last thirty five years has built his syndication investment company to over $300 million. His philosophy is to get rich slowly, buying value add properties and helping his investors make money.

This book gives you the methodologies, systems, strategies and processes to become a better real estate value investor. This book opens your eyes to new possibilities and ways to make money in today's real estate market. Get real life case studies and examples from leading investors in the Value Investor Profiles at the end of each chapter. There are many case studies showing how other people, just like you, are executing real estate value investing strategies.

## It's Time To Get In The Game

I am happy to have the privilege of offering you an inside look into the game of real estate value investing. My goal is to open your eyes to the possibilities of learning new ways to invest in real estate at one of the most important times in our country's history. We are sitting on the precipice of exciting times for value real estate investors. A few short years ago, value real estate investors struggled to find investments that made any economic sense. Real estate prices were inflated well above many standards of reasonableness. The investor herd mentality prevailed as real estate prices continued to climb to unprecedented heights. But, as things usually do, things changed.

A great credit crisis hit our country in late 2008, causing a severe collapse in both the residential and commercial real estate markets. The real estate market collapse led the economy into a deep recession. The U.S. unemployment rate soared to almost 10%, personal and business bankruptcies skyrocketed, real estate construction came to a halt, real estate foreclosures jumped to multi-decade highs, and real estate prices dropped by 50% in some areas of the country. The big real estate balloon popped, and did it pop!

Just like when real estate prices got too high at the peak in 2008, they now have gone down too low, well below replacement cost in many areas. The economy is picking back up again, demand for real estate is increasing and the job market is improving. My friends, this is a perfect set up for real estate value investors. Prices have fallen to the point that real estate deals pencil and make sense again. Value investors, it's time to get in the game.

Now is the time to lay our foundation for value creation. Now is the time to pick our spots. Now is the time to build our team of experts. Now is the time to rummage through the distress in the marketplace and find opportunities. Now is the time, my fellow value investors, to put on our Value Hound suits and get in the game.

- Craig Haskell, Value Hound
Haskell Value Real Estate Investor

# *How to Create Value Revitalizing Underperforming Distressed Apartments*

Carlos Vaz is Founder of The Conti Organization, a real estate investment company that specializes in buying underperforming apartment buildings in Dallas and Houston, Texas. Carlos started the Conti Organization in early 2008 at the young age of 30 and has built his real estate company to over 2,700 units. In short order, Carlos has purchased over 20 apartment properties, holding thirteen and flipping the other seven properties. Carlos tells how an immigrant from Brazil built his company with little resources, and how he quickly made contacts with investors to fund his real estate business.

I met Carlos at his second office, Maximo's Restaurant, in Dallas. He meets different people there almost every day for lunch where he eats and greets, talking mostly about investing in his deals.

**Tell us about your company, its business model, and your focus.**

I'd say the most important thing about the company itself is what we stand for. The name "Conti" actually was named after my mom, Neusa Conti. Our first project was in March of 2008. From March to now, we've closed two other projects last week, so that brought us close to 2,800 units. We are very focused on what we do, so in a nutshell, everything about Conti is only multifamily,

150-plus units, your typical B and C type in the four major cities: Dallas, Houston, San Antonio, and Austin. Of the 13 projects we have done, 12 of them were REO or distressed type of properties, and if they're distressed it's for a good reason. Our job is to really understand why they're called distressed and how we are able to turn that around.

**How do you position your company to take advantage of the opportunities today?**

I think the best way is to keep it simple. There are a lot of people that get into the market, and they want to talk a big game. They want to come, want to sit in a fund of $50 million, sit in a fund of $100 million, or have $20 million behind them. There's a saying here in Texas that we say, "All hat and no cattle." So basically people talk too much, but they're not able to perform. In our case, we don't say that we have $50 million. We have $20 million. We work extremely hard to close our projects, so the way to position ourselves better is to understand the market better than anyone else. We believe that we are the biggest asset – we as a company – and the deals, they have to feature our systems. The moment you try to change the company, you lose everything.

**Can you give us three or four things a deal must have to fit your portfolio?**

Well, it has to be over 150 units. Location – we're not going to go to the war zone. Since what we do is more like the blue collar type of property, what's important to us is high visibility. We want the property to be very close to a major highway, or if you're next door to a Home Depot or Walgreens, that's excellent. So, that's something important to us. Of course, the price we are paying. In a nutshell, I look at this project today, and if I see the NOI in a year or two after spending "X" amount in Capex (capital expenses), and if the NOI gives me a cap rate of more than 10, we have a deal.

**Carlos, your background is quite interesting. Can you tell us how you got started in this business?**

I lived in Boston for almost 10 years. I put myself through school during the night. I attended Harvard extension school in economics. During the day, I worked in construction, from being a laborer, carpenter, then a project manager. From early 2005 to early 2007, I started doing single family (homes) in the greater Boston area. I did approximately 34 projects. When things started to get better for me, the market started changing. So there was too much speculation in Boston. That's when I started selling my projects.

And the opportunity came to look into multifamily, through a friend of mine who had bought a 30-unit apartment building. I went to get my CCIM. Then when I went back to Boston, I said to myself that I needed to go somewhere else; somewhere that's growing. It was between North Carolina and Texas, and Texas became the best choice. Then it was between Dallas and Austin; Dallas became the best choice. I moved to Dallas in August of 2007. Once I got here, my job was to get to know as many people as I could.

**Did you have any mentors or people that helped you along the way?**

My mentors, first of all, they're always going to be my parents. I was attending NYU in New York. It was George Ross, who is Donald Trump's senior advisor. I was watching "The Apprentice" one day, and I saw him on the TV, and said, "Oh, I like that guy." I never cared about Trump, but I like him because that guy is so good, and the knowledge, and total negotiation. I did a search on him, and I saw that he had a book, and I bought his book. I was reading the book, and at the last page, he was a teacher at NYU. I thought, "Oh, that's interesting." I was checking NYU website, and two weeks later, he had a class that would start in negotiations. I was living in Boston; he is in New York, and I even thought twice, and so okay, I'm signing up. But it was crazy because I didn't have that much money back then, and then for almost six months, I had to get on a bus at 2:00 p.m. in Boston, get to New York at 6:00, run to NYU, attend the class, and wait for him, and then we would walk to the train station. Then I would get a bus back at 10:00 p.m., get to Boston at 2:00 a.m., and run to my job at 6:00 a.m.

**You closed your first deal, a 208-unit apartment investment back in March 2008, with basically few contacts, limited sources of capital, and little multifamily experience. How'd you get this deal done?**

It was very challenging. I think that the most challenge for any type of business is that people always put money first, mainly in multifamily. In multifamily, you're going to see $3 million or $4 million type of projects, and where is the money going to come from? Why are you concerned about the money? Because the money's going to get you the deal, but you're going to get the deal. If you stop everything and ask yourself, "Okay, I want to buy this project, but what am I going to offer to my investors? What am I going to offer to my partners?" Stop and put the money last, and put them first. So I think that the moment you're able to say, "What am I able to offer them," you are able to make more.

That project was very challenging because I just got to Dallas; I didn't know anyone; and it was kind of crazy. The whole kind of "make it happen" attitude – the need to find a way – well, the best thing that I saw about this project is it was – they were asking $4,290,000; they had an offer for $3.8 million. I saw an opportunity, and said, "If we put this property under contract, it's the end of the year, it's a bank owned property, they're going to be able to take this property from their books." And that's basically what they wanted to do.

To make a long story short, I was able to negotiate with the bank to get the deal as low as $3.1 million, which gave me a very steep discount. But you need to sell yourself to the broker to offer the deal. I was always out working; I met that broker at the Dallas Chamber of Commerce. But something that I always have with me is a one-page long business card, and it is very brief: This is Carlos Vaz. This is what I have done. This is what I want to do. So whenever I go to a meeting, I bring that with me and say, "Listen, this is what I'm thinking about doing," and consult on that work. So that broker, she believed in me. And then, I was looking for a project to build my team. I was looking for a CPA. That CPA – I met someone who was a CPA, and that CPA introduced me to one of my best friends here. He became a small investment partner, but since we were able to negotiate a good price, at the last minute, I was not able to find a partner. I started calling all the people who bought properties around the property. So then I found out that the guy who bought the property in front of this one, barely two months earlier, he paid about maybe $6,000 per unit more (for his property) than we were paying.

So I called him. That was the fastest call; I said, "Listen, this is who I am; this is what I've been thinking." I was able to get his information through a broker, and said, "I have this project; what is it you like to do?" He said, "Tell me about the project." "The project is across the street from yours." It was less than 10 minutes.

What was a drawback is that my ownership was nothing. So you talk about working for free. I mean, you're basically working for free. I mean, there's no way to compare where we were and where we are today. Today, as a company, we don't do anything with less than 30% of ownership. With many projects, we have 40, or 50. So even with that small ownership, how could I make the money? So doing extra marketing, extra everything because to me, it was an opportunity to learn about the business, and that was priceless.

**As you started buying more deals, you had to raise more money. What types of activities did you engage in to raise money from sources?**

The best way to raise capital is be prepared. We're constantly doing that. Keep it simple. And if you need to get a laptop to explain a deal, it's not a good deal. I mean, you need to keep it simple. I mean, of course, you're going to have all the legal documents; you're going to have all the projections – the five years and everything else, but in a nutshell, if you're not able to explain the project in barely three pages, maybe one, something's wrong. I mean, transparency is something extremely important to us. And the whole reference – being able to say, "Listen, go check about us. Go talk to some other investors." That's what we do now. A little bit different. Like people, we always give other investors references; we give our attorneys references; and go check on us.

I think the most important thing that people need to realize that you're dealing with people. Get out from the desk. Go meet the people, face-to-face. Go shake hands. Get out of the comfort zone. Emails don't work for that.

**How do you find the investors?**

The way I see it, it's talking to brokers about who bought a deal. Can I see your project? Let me see your project, then I want you to come and see mine. So that's a way I have been able to find people.

I used to speak at a lot of country clubs. There's the Dallas Country Club. They used to have a real estate club, and I used to attend – I attended five times, then they invited me to come back and speak. Sure. That's something that gives a little bit more credibility. So that's something that helps. I mean, you see a lot of marketing, a lot of PR is very strong, not because you want to be flashy and say, Conti, Conti, Conti. We, as a company, don't like the flashy stuff. We're very low-key. But all of the PR helps us to get new deals, and it helps the exposure to get new investors.

To raise the money, to have someone commit, and to do business with you, people have to like you and trust you. Only then will the money come.

**You found some great deals. That's helped you raise money, too, hasn't it?**

Sure. Well, see, that's what I'm saying. If you're not able to make yourself the asset first, how can you make yourself the asset?

Learn as much as you can about real estate. Learn as much as you can about the business itself, about the market.

## What kind of fees do you charge?

I have a 1% asset management fee. We just hired a new director of construction. I have a construction fee of 8 to 10 (percent), depending on the standing in a project, and an acquisition fee; some projects are 100 (thousand dollars); some projects are 150 (thousand dollars). And that's it.

## Of all the functions that you're involved with on a daily basis, from raising equity, sourcing new acquisitions, rehabbing properties, managing the properties, and so forth, what functions do you like doing best, and why?

I think that my best function, of course, negotiations. I love to negotiate. It's where my heart is. I love to put the things together because, to me, if you buy it right – 90% is buying right. After buying right, 98% is managing right. To negotiate, to put things together, that's really where my passion is. I like that a lot.

**Carlos Vaz**
Founder, The Conti Organization

Carlos Vaz is Founder of Conti Organization, a multifamily investment and asset management company based in Dallas, Texas that specializes in value-added class B and class C multifamily assets.

Carlos worked his way through college in Brazil studying law. At 19, he moved to the United States with $2,000 to his name, no friends or family in town, and no paying job. Carlos began buying single family investment properties in the Boston area where he bought and sold over 30 houses. He moved to Dallas in 2007 and started the Conti Organization. Since the acquisition of his first 208-unit apartment building in March of 2008, he has gone on to build a very successful apartment investment company with almost 3,000 units in his portfolio, all by the young age of 31.

# Chapter **1**

## *My First Deal as a*
## *Real Estate Value Investor*

*"There probably isn't another group in the country that's done 200 repositions. We don't do new development. It's strictly existing multifamily properties. We can buy them at big discounts to replacement cost and add value through our expertise."*

*Jerome Fink*
*The Bascom Group*

I always wanted to be in real estate. From my days in college at California University at Long Beach back in the late 70's, I was fascinated by investing in real estate. I feverishly read real estate investing books, went to seminars, and spoke with other investors about their real estate investments. At the very center of what intrigued me most was the large potential of making a lot of money investing in real estate without any money or credit, and only working a few hours a week.

After graduating from college in 1982, I attended a Robert Allen seminar, famous for his bestselling book *Nothing Down*, to learn how to invest in real estate without any money. Mr. Allen was a very compelling speaker with a successful system of buying property from owners who didn't want to be property owners any longer. He called these types of property owners, "Don't Wanters."

Don't Wanters are property owners who are very motivated to quickly sell their properties to solve a business or personal problem. Don't Wanters sell their properties using creative financing so that an investor doesn't need to put any money down to buy the property, and many times, can get money back at closing. I thought, "Wow, with a little bit of energy and hard work, I could find Don't Wanters and become a real estate investor."

I was young and had nothing to lose so without a lot of knowledge or experience, I decided to use the Robert Allen Nothing Down system and get my piece of the American dream. I created an investment company, Paramount Investment Company, whose sole focus was to buy distressed properties in Southern California from Don't Wanters.

Searching for Don't Wanters became my obsession. I contacted bank REO departments, worked with real estate agents, sent out mailings to out-of-state property owners, advertised for motivated property owners, and contacted property owners whose mortgages were going into default. I was on a mission to find distressed real estate to buy and nothing was going to get in my way.

I spent about eight months searching for Don't Wanters and made lots of offers to buy from leads that I generated. I was starting to get frustrated that I still had not bought a property. Most of the feedback I had received from sellers and agents was that my offers contained little substance in the way of financial commitment. Properties were being sold to other buyers that were more qualified. My frustrations lead to concern about the viability of my business plan.

Another seminar was coming to town so I thought, "I must be doing something wrong so getting more education was the answer." I attended a seminar put on by Wade Cook. His system focused on buying properties that were in distress and quickly selling them using creative financing. In essence, an investor would buy a property with little to no down payment and assume the existing debt. Then the investor would sell the property to another buyer for a higher price using an All Inclusive Mortgage, also known as a "Wrap Around Mortgage." The theory was that the investor would get a cash down payment from the new buyer and create an equity spread between the underlying mortgages and the Wrap Around Mortgage creating a monthly income stream. Do this multiple times on properties and monthly income stream builds.

This seminar got me recharged and energized to find deals. I went back out into the marketplace looking for distressed deals that fit the Wade Cook system. Using similar methods to flush out deals that fit my criteria, I spent tireless hours searching and negotiating deals. Again, I was pushed back with resistance from sellers and property owners. I was confused as to why I was having so much trouble succeeding when I was reading and hearing others have so much success.

After almost two years of trying to buy an investment property, I finally realized that the good deals were available but the market dynamics required a cash down payment. Distressed property owners were in the market, but they were selling to other investors that gave them cash. Why would a seller take my no down deal when they had the option to sell to a buyer that gave them cash?

I loved the real estate business so much that in 1984 I decided to learn the business the correct way. I got my real estate license and pursued employment with a professional real estate company. Having been burned by the real estate seminar hucksters in the single family arena, I wanted a more professional and sophisticated real estate career, so I took a job in commercial real estate industry as a commercial real estate agent with a specialization in the office space.

Understanding leasing office space, leases and building management set a great foundation for my career. On a daily basis, I was dealing with professional and sophisticated real estate investors and owners helping them buy, lease and manage their commercial real estate investments. I learned something interesting. None of the professional investors I worked with ever bought their properties using no money down techniques. What I learned was that more than 70% of professional investors use other people's money (OPM) to raise the equity funds to buy investment property. They create an investment group and pool other investors' money together to buy real estate. If you look around, the biggest and most successful real estate investors such as Donald Trump, Sam Zell, and others create investment groups to buy their properties. They don't fly by the seat of their pants operating on a shoe string budget.

## I'm in The Real Estate Investing Game

In 1986, my real estate value investing career finally found success because I now knew how to play the game like the professionals. Every Sunday, the *LA Times* newspaper published a list of Veteran Administration (VA) foreclosed single family homes. On weekends, I plotted houses on my Thomas Guide Map and drove to each house to inspect the condition. I walked each house estimating the cost to repair the house into a re-saleable condition. Houses that looked like a good deal, I would pull sale comps in the area. Finally, I would crunch the numbers to evaluate the profit potential after purchase price, renovation and carrying costs. A house that gave me at least a 30% profit potential, I made offers on.

It was tough buying VA foreclosure homes because, as an investor, I was competing with buyers who would use and live in the house. These types of buyers could afford to pay a higher price than an investor, like me, who was looking to make a profit. However, I knew finding a great deal was critical for me to attract investors.

After about two months of making lots of offers, I finally got an offer accepted from the VA. Yes! I had an accepted agreement to buy my first investment property. All the hard work had paid off. Now, I had to figure out the process to get this deal closed.

The house I had under contract was in the Southern California submarket of Chino, California. The house was a two story, 2,200 square foot home with four bedrooms and two baths located in a good neighborhood next to a public golf course. The purchase price was $70,000 all cash with a cash down payment of $21,000 and a new first mortgage of $49,000 from Sterling Savings and Loan. The inspection period was 7 days with a closing period of 45 days. All-in-all, this was a good deal because the house only needed cosmetic repairs of $2,000, and the local sale comps were $115,000 leaving a nice profit of over $30,000.

Since I needed to find an investor to help fund the deal, I created a detailed investor information package to show investors.

The package included details about the house, the local market, a renovation budget, cost required to carry the property for six months, various fees associated with the closing and a short business plan. Creating the investor package took me a couple of days to complete.

I was really excited because I found such a great deal with the opportunity to make an investor and myself a lot of money. What I later learned, after doing many value add investments, was that my enthusiasm about the great deal was quite infectious. Investors that I brought the deal to also became excited because they could see how much money they were going to make. Finding an investor to help fund the cash down payment on the Chino house was much easier than I expected. Enthusiasm, a business plan, and a profitable deal bring investors out of the woodwork to play in the real estate game.

From my job, I was able to save some money so I wanted to put my own money into the deal. I found a partner, Reid, to put up 50% of the funds needed to execute our business plan, and I put up the other 50%. We both were equal partners and shared in all the duties to complete the renovation, handle the house operations and management, and eventually sell the house.

Reid and I met at the escrow company to close on the house purchase. Because property taxes and mortgage interest are paid in arrears, we had a nice credit on the closing statement leaving cash balance due from the buyers of $19,800. Reid and I each provided escrow with a cashier's check in the amount of $9,900. We both left the escrow company excited and pumped up on our new purchase.

Having never done a partnership before and being relatively young and inexperienced, we did not have a written partnership agreement. This deal was done the old fashion way, on a hand shake. Was this a smart thing to do? No. Would I do it again? No. But hey, it's not pretty when you get going without a road map.

The Chino house closed on Friday. Reid, his brother (I can't remember his name) and I met at the house first thing the following Saturday morning. His brother was a construction contractor and was tasked with completing the renovation work.

All three of us created a plan to renovate the property. Property renovations included exterior trim paint, landscaping, interior wall repairs, interior paint, bathroom and miscellaneous plumbing repairs, and general clean up; nothing too major. We made a list of supplies and went to the hardware store to purchase the items on our list. Our plan was to begin construction work on Monday and have the house completely renovated within two weeks.

First thing Monday morning many problems sprang up. Reid and his brother lived at the north end of the San Fernando Valley, creating an almost two hour drive to the Chino house. Our construction guy didn't show up until almost 1pm. And when he did finally show up, there was no electric for him to use his power tools. Turns out the power company rep hadn't been out to turn on the power. Needless to say, little work was completed on our first day.

Day two starts out the same way. Again, our construction guy doesn't show up until 2pm. The electric power has been turned on so Reid's brother can use his power tools. By the end of the day, we made some mild progress, but I'm starting to worry about meeting our two week planned renovation schedule.

Big problems happen the third day. I called the gas company to have the gas turned on so that we could complete some work, including adding a new water heater. The gas company said that since the house sat vacant for such a long time before my purchase, they had to remove the gas meter from the house. Here's the real kicker; before the gas meter could be re-installed, the City of Chino had to inspect and approve a Certificate of Occupancy. I knew this couldn't be good.

I called the city planning department and requested an inspection of the house as per the directions from the gas company. Turned out the city was busy and it would take 7-days before the city inspector could make it to the house. Ouch!

When the city inspector finally arrived, he conducted a thorough and complete investigation of the house. His findings weren't good. To get a clean bill of health, the house needed some electrical work completed, plumbing repaired, and the water heater, which was in the garage, needed to be built up 2 feet off the ground and secured to the wall. I started to stress out about the additional cost and time requirements to meet our plan.

Reid's brother could handle the work, but the costs would increase. The additional cost would increase by $2,500, taking the total cost to almost $5,000, well over our planned budget of $2,000. While this didn't sit well with us, we knew that because we bought the house cheap enough, there was a little room for mistakes.

We are now a week and a half into the renovation with some new surprises from the city. It's clear that the renovation is going to take much longer; and longer it did. Reid's brother wouldn't show up for days on end creating delays. The stress continues to build on the investment because the longer the process took, the more it costs in carrying costs. Even though it conflicts with our regular jobs, Reid and I decided to handle some of the lighter construction work ourselves. We could do some painting, add wood paneling, add landscaping, and clean up; so we did.

It's now one month into the renovation and we are almost done. This was supposed to be a quick cosmetic renovation, but it turned into more than we expected. The list of repairs the city inspector gave us was completed so we schedule him to come back out to approve our Certificate of Occupancy.

Another week goes by before the city inspector shows up. Thankfully, his review of the repairs and property gives us a green light to get our Certificate of Occupancy. I immediately call the gas company to install the gas meter so that we can install a new gas water heater.

As history often times does, it repeats itself. Reid's brother is nowhere to be found to install the hot water heater. After lots of hounding and two days later, Reid's brother finally shows up to install the water heater and complete all the renovations. In the end, it took six weeks to complete the house renovation with total renovation costs at $6,500, well over our two week schedule and renovation budget of $2,000.

## Time to Sell and Make a Profit

Now, it's finally time to sell the house to capture our profit. The process to get the house in saleable condition didn't go quite as planned so we were glad to be onto the next phase. Getting the house listed was our next step.

We drove the market looking for other houses for sale. As we drove, we looked for properties that had real estate agent "for sale" signs on them. Our mission was to find the name of the real estate agent who had the most signs up in the local area. After spending a few hours driving, we found a lady from Century 21 (can't remember her name either) that had three times as many signs as any other real estate agent.

We contacted the Century 21 agent and set up an appointment to list the house for sale. When we arrived at her office, she had printed off the sale comps of houses for sale in the area where our house was located. The average sale comps were $115,000. We listed the house with the Century 21 agent for six months at $120,000, paying a 6% real estate commission.

Unfortunately, the house did not sell quickly. One month had gone by with no offers so we lowered the listing price to $115,000. Another three months went by with only one low ball offer that we declined. It had been four months and we were starting to get nervous. We decided to lower the listing price to $110,000.

There were no calls from our real estate agent as her six month listing was getting ready to expire. Then, two weeks before her listing agreement was set to expire, we got a call for our agent telling us we had an offer. She was representing a male buyer who was in a wheelchair, and the house works out well for him because of the huge downstairs area. The offer was for $104,000 all cash. We tell the agent that it's too low, but we will consider it and get back to her.

Reid and I spent some time considering the offer and our investment situation. From a big picture standpoint, it was costing us lots of money to carry the house. It had been six months with little buyer activity, and we were eager to get the property sold. In the end, our decision was to take the buyer's offer price on the condition our real estate agent would cut her real estate commission in half. Instead of getting a full commission of roughly $6,200, she would get a half of commission of about $3,100. With the house listing ready to expire, we felt we had some leverage to get our agent to accept our proposal. And after taking a day to consider the proposal, our agent accepted our proposal of the reduced commission.

The escrow period was pretty quick taking only 30 days. The buyer already had financing lined up so he was able to close quickly. Almost seven months later from the time we bought the investment house, the Chino house closed escrow completing the entire process. The escrow company gave us a check in the amount of $22,300, which Reid and I split 50/50.

## Lessons Learned From My First Real Estate Value Investment

There were a lot of feelings I experienced during my first real estate value investment. Anytime you do something new without proper guidance and direction, it creates numerous emotions that eventually lead to a negative psychological thought process creating stress and pressure. I made a lot of mistakes on my first real estate deal but learned a lot from the process. While I did make some money, the learning process was invaluable. Talk about the school of hard knocks; I got a true lesson from the street.

Whether you are a new real estate investor working on a $100,000 single family investment or an experienced investor working on a $10 million commercial real estate investment, many of the lessons contained in my story are relevant to your success. Let's take a look at some lessons I learned:

- There is no quick and easy way to achieve success in the game of real estate value investing. Make sure you have the proper professional training and guidance before getting in the game.

- It takes real money to safely invest in real estate. If you don't have any, partner with others that do. Having money presents real estate value investors MANY more opportunities, especially if you want to do multiple deals.

- Finding a great deal is at the very core of buying real estate value investments.

- Keep your investments simple. Find a great deal, find investors, add or create value, and then hold or sell the property for a profit.

- Conduct a complete and thorough investigation of the property's physical condition, operations, and financial condition. Avoid surprises.

- Surround yourself with the very best experts who know what they are doing. Taking short cuts usually ends up costing more time and money.

- Prepare a partnership agreement and supporting documents with all your investors that spells out in detail what is expected of everyone.

- Make sure you are fairly compensated in the way of fees or profit splits from your investment partnership. I spent much more time through the entire process of my first investment where I invested half of the equity capital and only got 50% of the proceeds.

- Invest in local markets you understand, and that are not located too far away from home base.

- Develop a business plan and a financial model that spell out the details of the investment. Use worse case scenarios in your financial model. Plan to spend more on capital improvements that take longer to complete. Be conservative with your financial model by planning for rental income to be lower and operating expenses to be higher than you first think.

- Plan for more capital reserves than you expect. Add 20% extra to what you initially plan for reserves.

It's an ongoing challenge to become well disciplined investors because our emotions, greed, or pressures from others, whether personal or business, lead us to overlook best practice principles. I know of some of the most experienced investors in the world that are too aggressive when modeling their deals, hire friends or family instead of getting the best experts, buy rental property in markets they have little knowledge about, hire poor property management companies or fail to adequately plan for sufficient capital reserves.

While the basic principles I've outlined above may seem to be quite elementary and only applicable to new investors, experienced investors can save and make more money by realizing and implementing best practice principles

# How to Reposition Multifamily Properties for Maximum Income and Growth

Jerry Fink originally started his company, The Bascom Group, with the goal of only buying 500 units in the Southern California area. But since 1996, Jerry's company has bought and sold over 52,000 multifamily units totaling in excess of $6 billion, completed 199 property renovations, and generated over 45% IRR's. In this interview, Jerry uncovers the methodology and strategies they use to reposition distressed multifamily properties for maximum income and growth. Learn the inside details on why Jerry has been so successful.

**Tell us about The Bascom Group, its focus and business model.**

Our focus is value add, multifamily, and distressed multifamily assets. They're apartments that we can acquire at significant discounts to replacement cost, where we can add our operational expertise to lower expenses, improve revenue, and improve the quality of the asset, with the goal to make an internal rate of return in the high teens over a five-year hold to our investors.

Our business strategy is to really pursue distressed and value add multifamily deals throughout the U.S. They're all existing properties, typically cash-flowing properties, and properties that have operational challenges or higher-than-market vacancy, high expenses, tougher tenant profiles, and deferred maintenance. We'll find those properties typically off-market or through our contacts, and then put in money, expertise, and operational improvements to improve the earnings.

## How did you get started in this business?

We got started in 1996. My two partners are David Kim and Derek Chen. We all went to school together at the University of Wisconsin where we all went through the real estate program there. After five years of working in the institutional world, we put together a business plan, where our goal was to acquire only 500 units in Orange County.

We saw the opportunity back in 1995-96 when California had gone through another down-cycle. There was a tremendous amount of foreclosures and distressed assets, so David Kim and I put together a business plan, presented it to Derek Chen, another one of our classmates, and formed the The Bascom Group, which is named after Bascom Hill at the University of Wisconsin.

So, we formed our company with fairly modest intentions to only acquire 500 units, and our first deal was a 58-unit $2 million property. It was a home savings foreclosure. We bought it, raised the equity, painted it, improved the interiors and landscaping, repositioned it, and sold it for a pretty significant profit. We just took that success and continued to buy more properties throughout Orange County, and then eventually expanded into San Diego, the Inland Empire, L.A. County, Seattle, Northwest San Francisco, opened up an office in Arizona, and an office in Texas as well.

We grew our company over the years by bringing in additional people and expanding with regional offices. We typically would go to markets where we would see distressed economies or fundamentals, and where we've had the most success is really being a contrarian buyer in down markets. And so all these markets have gone through different cycles at different points in time, and as they've bottomed, we've generally ramped up and gone to certain markets and been very active buyers and reposition experts.

**So you buy the markets first, and then look for distressed opportunities?**

Yes. We focus on markets that are good markets – meaning, they are desirable areas, where they've got long-term population and job growth prospects, and our goal really is to pursue those markets where they're places that people want to be. They want to live there. They've got good school systems, good job-creators. But, they're in a down-cycle where they may have had a tech economy issue or they've had some kind of national economy problem, but it's a cycle problem; it's not a long-term issue. We look for those distressed markets, and we try to find those markets where the existing sellers are interested in selling because they've been so beaten up by the downturn. That's where we can come in with new capital, a new business plan and reposition those properties.

**Bascom has had tremendous success. Can you give us an idea on how you've done $6 billion of business over the last 14 years?**

I think it was a function of doing the same thing repeatedly, very well. We've tried to turn our business into a merchant building of value add and distressed repositions. My partner David Kim, who handles the operational renovation aspect of our company, has done an excellent job of really finding ways to quickly assemble great teams to manage the properties, to reposition, and to increase earnings. The goal is to get in there as quickly as we can, put in new management, finish the renovations within less than a year, rebrand the property, and then push the earnings up over the course of several years.

The reason for our growth and our success has been that we brought on a number of additional partners who are very seasoned professionals in the industry who have helped us expand, and we've given them the ability to not only take the responsibility, but they have the authority to manage their regions and their deals.

**Why is The Bascom Group different or unique?**

We are different from most groups because we've got teams of people that are specialized in a number of certain responsibilities and authorities. We've got dedicated renovation managers and dedicated people that focus on expenses. We have people that specialize in revenue. And these people have done 100, 150, 200 renovations, repositions, or management takeovers, so they're very experienced at what they do. Again, as I've talked about, it's almost like a merchant building factory.

The second way we're different is our experience. There probably isn't another group in the country that's done 200 repositions. We don't do new development. It's strictly existing multifamily properties. We can buy them at big discounts to replacement cost and add value through our expertise.

Third, we give people not only a lot of responsibility, but a lot of authority to make decisions. So the people here are empowered to do things.

Fourth, we've also reorganized our company by teams, where these teams have not only acquisition people, but operational personnel as well. We've created annual competitions and incentives where their goal is, "How much can I drive revenue? How much can I lower expenses? How much can I increase NOI?" Every quarter, we meet and we discuss those targets and objectives, and we put the teams against each other. We might have a Texas team versus an Atlanta team, and their goal is to meet the market standards or beat each other on lowering expenses. And then, we provide bonuses based on their performance.

And the fifth thing is, every employee and partner here at Bascom puts money in these deals. Every employee is a partner in all of our deals. Our people may have $100,000 in or they may have $1,000 in, but they have material amounts of their own net worth invested so they're incentivized to make it work because they've got their net worth on the line, too.

## Is there a sample or an example of something you've done recently?

We bought a Class A asset that had about $130,000 a unit of debt on the property. It cost $150,000 a unit to build today, and we bought the property for $100,000 a unit, and then we put on a Freddie Mac acquisition reposition loan.

The property was built in 2002. We spent about $7,000 a unit in upgrades. It was a Class A building and the only challenge was it just had too much debt on the property. We repainted the exterior, changed the name, rebranded the building, upgraded the interiors, converted a storage room into a movie theater, enhanced the gym, put a putting green in, and built a better tot lot.

We took this building that was probably an A-, B+ building, seven years old, which was very nice, and really turned it into an A+ quality building in a sub-market, and our total basis was $108,000 a unit. That building today would cost $150,000 a unit to build. We feel like we've got a very high-quality asset at 70% of replacement cost in an A location. It's done very well since then.

## How do you find great deals?

We are sourcing them through a variety of ways. One is the traditional brokerage community, which is 80-90% of all transactions. That is listed deals. They're deals that the owner hired a broker to do a limited marketing and we're pursuing those.

We are also making unsolicited offers on markets that we want to be in. For example, we'll go to Las Vegas or Phoenix to find some markets and we'll send out unsolicited offers on all the buildings we want to buy. And we not only will send those offers to the owners, but we'll send those offers to the lenders.

So we'll make unsolicited offers to buy the debt on properties because we've got databases that will tell us what the rents are. We know what the expenses are, we can easily tell what the values are, and we can also find out who the lender is to contact. We'll make offers to buy the loan, we'll make offers to buy the property, and we'll see who shakes out first.

Third, we've got a number of sources that will broker us loans. Every day we probably get half a dozen opportunities shown to buy notes on properties. We're looking at a lot of those opportunities as well.

Then fourth, our existing lenders and partners are coming to us, saying, "Hey, I've got this challenged property," or "I've got a sponsor that I don't like anymore. Can you come in and take over the position? Let's re-cut a new basis, create a new structure of profits and splits, and reposition the deal as if I'm starting over."

**Most of your properties go through a remodeling process. What capital improvement items give the most "bang for the buck" on rent increases?**

I believe that most of the cosmetic items give the biggest bang for the buck. It's the exterior paint and landscaping because those, as a total cost relative to your basis, are fairly modest. So if you can repaint the exterior, put some new signage in, improve the landscaping, that has a tremendous impact on the physical appeal from someone driving down the street.

And then second, once that person enters the property, you get the most bang for the buck by really upgrading the amenities. You can put in a tot lot or playground that might cost $40,000. But if you're buying a $20 million deal, it's only a fraction of the total cost basis. And, if you've got families with kids, which is very popular today, and the two to six-year-olds see that little playground, they want to live there.

We put in other amenities as well, like gyms. A gym might cost you $30,000 to $50,000. We're finding today that that's incredibly important because people are canceling their gym memberships. So the old model used to be, when you put amenities in, they're great for marketing, but no one uses them. We're finding now that people not only want to use them, they need to use them because they're canceling their cable bill; they're canceling their Internet service; they're canceling their gym membership. They're really cutting back their expenses during the recession and so now they're using the gym onsite.

They're also using the business center. With business centers you will spend $10,000 to $15,000. Again, we used to build them with the intent that they look good but no one uses them. We're now finding most of our properties have a waiting list for people to get in to use the computers. And we always thought that everyone's got a computer in their apartment; they've got internet. Today we're finding they want to save that 50 bucks on internet service, and so they will go and spend a couple of hours in our computer room, using our computers.

So amenities are a big bang for the buck because when you add up the cost of it relative to your basis, it's a pretty small percentage, but it gives you a big bang for the buck.

We'll upgrade the leasing office, too, so when you walk in the leasing office, we'll bring it to an "A" quality standard, and we can do that, really, for a fraction of the price to build one new. We'll upgrade the leasing office so that when you walk in, it looks like a Class "A" facility with all the new amenities.

When the person goes to their unit, the first thing they see is we've upgraded the flooring. Now we're using this faux wood flooring, which are really vinyl sheets that look like distressed wood. If you've seen it, I mean you look at it and it looks like real wood. Sometimes we'll do the faux wood flooring. They've got countertops now that look like real granite. I walk in, I can't tell the difference. It's a faux granite countertop that's really Formica, which is an amazing product at a very cheap price. The old motto was, you put real granite in there and got this premium, and that doesn't work anymore. So we do the faux granite and the faux wood floors. We'll sometimes paint the cabinets, occasionally put in new appliances. But our interiors right now, it's really improving appearance with flooring, some paint, and accent walls.

Also our models, we really make our models look amazing. So we've got nice little children's rooms, the right kind of tone in there. We'll put in flowers, plants, paintings on the wall, the nice scents, and play the nice music. We turn our models into really nice quality looking units. We find that if you've got the great exterior, got the great leasing office with amenities, and they walk into these interiors, and they've got an accent wall with the right decorations and the right appeal, then we've really got a product that can outsell the competition, and again, at a fraction of the cost.

### Do you leave some kind of value component for the next buyer?

The smart value-add operator never does 100%. The next buyer can assume or believe they're going to get some additional rent increase or additional rent pop by doing these additional improvements. Everyone always wants to feel like they're going to add some improvements or add their expertise. They need that story to sell to their lender or their investor that they're going to run it better and going to raise the rents. They can pay a cap rate that may be lower than you can ever imagine because they've got NOI or an income stream higher than we do. And so you want to give them that ability that there is additional upside, and so we never do 100% of what we really should do.

### How long does it take to turn a deal and reposition it from renovations through lease-up?

You can do the physical enhancements on the exterior within a year. To do the interiors, it takes two to three years, but it also takes time to push the rents up because you never really raise everyone's rent to market day one because the shock of that might vacate the building. Typically, we'll raise rents in sequence over a three-year period on existing residents so that the amount of increase is not such a shock that they move out of the building. On new units that are renovated, we'll ask market, but existing units, we'll transition them to market over a period of time.

### Are there certain capital items that you start first versus some you start later?

You should always start from the top down, meaning you do the roof first; you do the siding second; you do the landscaping third because you don't want your roofers wrecking your landscaping. So you should start kind of big picture exterior items, starting from top to bottom.

The goal, obviously, is to get the leasing office and amenities online first because you want to be able to sell your product. You want to get that leasing office, the new signage, amenities online quickly so that you can be up and running. You can do projects on the exterior of the property later, but you want to get that main entry done right away because that's what the consumer sees driving into your property.

## What value add strategies are you implementing now in this market?

We're out there looking at things that can bring us consumers and residents by spending very few dollars, and that are good for the community. That's part of our Triple Bottom Line program that we've developed. Dave Kim years ago realized that we've got these huge leasing offices that have been renovated, and they've got big clubhouse areas; they've got big meeting areas and amenities – that for the most part are really not being utilized. We discovered that, hey, we've got a captive 1,000 sometimes 3,000 or 4,000 people living in one of these communities. Why not take resume-building teachers, English teachers, job fairs, immigration seminars. You name it, let's create classes onsite that residents can go to and invite their friends.

We're finding that these residents will invite friends that don't live in our property. We're bringing people in that will go listen to a speaker on how to do better in sports, how to do your resume, or how to find a job. They'll go to our property and go, "Wow, this is a really nice property. Maybe I should live here." So it's a great way to generate traffic from your sub-market, and most of these services are for relatively low cost or free because they're non-profit groups, and they just need space to do that.

We've given apartments to teachers and security people and other groups like that, that can come in and do programs and teach people certain skills, and in return, we give them a discounted or free unit, and we think that's great because with all this vacancy today, you've got – in a typical building – 10 to 50 or 100 vacant units. It's really unused currency so why not take that unused currency, give it to a teacher or somebody else, and they'll go teach their class and now we've got happy residents that want to stay there, that want to bring their friends onsite. We think that's a great thing for the community and the building as well.

**To fund the equity portion of your deals, what sorts of activities – raising money activities – are you engaging in?**

We have got two groups of money. We have institutional programmatic joint ventures, where institutions have allocated a certain amount of capital to us to pursue a platform or program of acquisitions. Second, we have a network of high-net-worth individuals that are looking for certain types of transactions. So right now, there hasn't been a challenge of raising money necessarily; it's been more finding enough good opportunities that are out there. We're in this environment where there's plenty of capital, but we need more distressed deals.

**How do you typically structure your joint ventures?**

Our typical joint venture is structured where we put up anywhere from 5 to 10% of the equity, and our partner puts up anywhere from 90 to 95% of the equity. So every deal, we've got our own money in the deal, pari passu, and so we typically structure it where we put up our, say, 5 or 10%, they put up their 90-95%. We have a minimum preferred return anywhere from 6 to, say, 10%. After the preferred return is paid, we then go into a profits flip mode, anywhere from 50/50 to 70/30, to 60/40, depending on the investor and the deal. We're side by side with the investor, and we only participate in the profits until the investor has had a return on their capital or a return of their capital. So we feel like we're aligned with our investor to really maximize the profit, and again, we only participate when they've got their money back and return on it.

## Jerome Fink
Co-Founder, The Bascom Group

The Bascom Group (named after "Bascom Hill," upon which the University of Wisconsin Business School sits) was founded by three University of Wisconsin alumni, Derek Chen, Jerome Fink, and David Kim in 1996 in the midst of the savings and loan meltdown. Their business plan was to acquire and re-position 300 to 500 unit apartment buildings in the midst of the foreclosure and job crisis of the early 1990s in California by creating value-added renovations and community outreach programs.

Since then, Jerry Fink and Bascom have gone on to acquire 52,911 apartment units within 199 redevelopments and 3.1 million square feet of industrial and office properties, totaling in excess of $6.01 billion in transaction volume. Bascom has generated 45.90% leveraged property IRR's with a multiple of capital of 2.61x in an average of 2.95 year holding period on properties sold.

# Chapter **2**

## *Cashing in on Today's "Once in a Lifetime" Buying Opportunity*

*"I believe we are now in a "bottoming out" period, and we are going to see some earlier indicators of improvement (values increasing, a pick-up in leasing activity, an increased investor interest, and improving fundamentals)."*

Christopher E. Lee
CEL & Associates

You need to get in the real estate investment game...Today!  Most real estate is on sale at bargain prices in many markets. Real estate prices have become so cheap that there is no better time, as a real estate value investor, to cash in on today's fantastic buying opportunity.

The three most important things in real estate are timing, timing, and timing! According to the many informative and educational books by some of the industry's leading experts, the best real estate investment strategy will most likely fail if executed at the wrong time in the real estate cycle.  Timing the real estate market is the most critical component to the impact on the performance of your real estate profits.

For almost thirty years, I have been in the real estate game buying, owning, and managing over 7,000 units and 2.8 million square feet of commercial space, and providing advisory services on over $2 billion in value.  I have owned or managed many types of properties from single family homes to office buildings to retail centers to industrial buildings. I have watched decades of real estate cycles exhibit similar patterns where there were boom and bust cycles that greatly affected the wealth for me and my investors. The biggest profits were made in the boom cycle and the biggest losses were in the bust cycle.

Back in the 1990's, during the last real estate market crash, I was buying real estate value investments. My investors and I made six times our money within an average of 5 years. In today's most recent crash, we have suffered negative investment returns because of poor investment timing. While our properties performed better than the market, we still continued to struggle.

Over the years, I have learned some very tough lessons that have helped me create some valuable principles of value real estate investing. Investors should become more aggressive buyers of real estate when the market has crashed, similar to today's environment. The downside risk to investors' performance is limited while the upside potential is maximized, creating solid risk adjusted returns. On the flip side, value investors should become very conservative when the real estate market nears the peak of the cycle. Timing the real estate cycles is the most critical factor in determining the success or failure of a real estate investment.

## The Impact of Real Estate Cycles on Investment Performance

It may be the most important strategic concept to deal with in the investment world for contrary investors who seek to maximize wealth, outperform the competition and beat the market averages.

In many growing regions of the country, there is substantial opportunity to improve investment performance from careful analysis of real estate cycles. You have heard the old adage, "Buy low and sell high." Well, using a contrarian approach by analyzing real estate cycles can help you pick the best times to buy and sell real estate for maximum risk adjusted returns.

Contrary investing works in any market because human nature is the same everywhere. Most people are followers, not leaders. In the real estate investment market, the "herd" waits to buy until they see other investors buying and the "herd" waits to sell until they see other investors selling. As a result, the "herd" buys after prices have already risen, and sells after prices have already fallen.

Contrary real estate investors understand where we are in the real estate cycle so that they know when to buy low and when to sell high. Understanding and analyzing real estate cycles is the very foundation of contrary investing.

Since 1970, Maxwell Drever along with his companies, Drever Partners and Concierge Asset Management, has consistently used real estate cycles to maximize returns for himself and his investors. Mr. Drever has spent most of the past four decades fishing at the bottom of real estate market cycles.

Mr. Drever first began purchasing apartment properties in Seattle in the early 1970's when massive layoffs at the aerospace company Boeing Co. ravaged the city's economy. In 1987, amid plunging oil prices and employment, he bought apartments in Houston. And in the early 1990's, Mr. Drever purchased apartment properties in Phoenix from the Resolution Trust Corp., which had been set up by the federal government to sell off assets of insolvent savings and loans. His strategy has been simple and consistent: "Buy underperforming, well-located properties at the bottom of the real estate market in rebounding overbuilt markets, and reposition them to take advantage of the forthcoming growing market."

## What are Real Estate Cycles?

Everything in the world around us operates in cycles. The sun rises and it sets. The ocean tide comes in and goes out. The seasons change. People are born and they die. The real estate market is no different. Real estate cycles exist in both residential and commercial property markets. There are national and local real estate cycles that are affected by different economic, financial, and demographic factors. Understanding what drives the ups and downs of the real estate cycle can prove valuable to investors and others seeking to profit from real estate markets.

Cycles are common throughout the economy, not just in real estate. Individual industries, and sometimes the entire national economy, tend to swing from periods of "expansion" to periods of "contraction." From a real estate perspective, if the local economy is booming, demand for developed space will increase. Likewise, when recession hits, the demand for space decreases.

Over a period of many years, real estate experiences periods of excess demand ("hot" markets or seller's markets), which invariably are followed by periods of excess supply ("slow" markets or buyer's markets). These swings define a market real estate cycle. If new supply of space could be produced or withdrawn instantaneously, the market would always be in equilibrium, and there would be no cycle. But in reality, a considerable lag exists between the time demand for more housing or office space is identified and the time new space becomes available. This lag is a major part of what creates cycles.

Consider what happens when a local industry expands. Population grows as people are attracted to the area from other parts of the country. As local companies expand, they need more office or industrial space to grow their companies. Demand increases for real estate, disrupting the balance of supply and demand. It takes time for developers to recognize and respond to the increased real estate demand, and even more time to plan, finance, approve and complete new real estate projects such as office buildings, industrial buildings, retail centers, apartment communities, and/or houses. This is the "expansion phase" of the cycle.

Building too many new projects eventually catches up with and then surpasses the demand for these projects. Psychology plays a role in this over-correction because market expansions typically reward risk takers, increasing the developer's tendencies to overestimate potential demand. This "contraction" phase brings the market back to equilibrium. If new supply continues to come into the market after demand has begun to diminish, the cycle may enter a down or recession phase, driving down occupancy, rental rates and values.

## The Herd Mentality

Stoken in 1993 came up with the theory of The Herd Mentality:

"Following an extended period of strong expansion and prosperity, the "herd" adopts the psychology of affluence and its byproduct, economic optimism, wherein they enjoy life, have fun, and become economic risk takers. The "herd" mentality of optimism, once set off, takes on a life of its own and continues until the "herd" becomes excessively optimistic.

They rationalize that what has happened will continue to happen, and thus come to see less risk than actually exists. Consequently, the "herd" becomes risk takers, which in turn creates the conditions for a big bust. This bust, or recession, then sets off a psychology of pessimism, which continues until the "herd" sees more risk than really exists. At that point, the "herd" becomes risk averters, and lays the foundation for a long period of economic expansion."

If investors consistently buy into fear and sell into euphoria or greed, they'll make money. It sounds easy, but in practice, investors seldom do it. When everyone thinks that rents, occupancies and/or prices are going to crash, we tend to be afraid. When everyone is thrilled with the market, the excitement tends to rub off on us. Most of us don't like to stand-alone, clinging to an opinion that nearly everyone else seems to disagree with.

When people get caught up in a crowd, they stop thinking rationally and allow themselves to be governed almost entirely by emotions. This state of mind prevails at nearly all important market tops and bottoms. Almost everyone is convinced that the market will keep going up – or down – with no end in sight.

Unfortunately, the market never accommodates a crowd for long. It can't. If the market did what virtually everyone expected it to do, making money would be easy. As a bruised and scarred veteran of the "battle for investment survival" will tell you, life doesn't work quite that way. In fact, it's logically impossible for the market to follow the path that an overwhelming majority of investors believe it will take. A contrarian investor looks for important market reversals when the overwhelming majority of investors expect the prevailing trend to continue.

Timing the real estate market cycles has been the very foundation of Sam Zell's contrarian investment philosophy. Sam Zell likes tough times where pessimism is everywhere, and has long modeled himself as a contrarian. This philosophy made him a billionaire. That was back in the late 1980's when the commercial real estate business was in ruins after a frenzy of overbuilding spawned by weird tax shelters and the savings and loan crisis. Shrewd and tough, Zell smelled opportunity. He bought up scores of properties at bargain prices from distressed owners. He was nicknamed, "The Grave Dancer."

## Cycle "Lag"

Fueled by the "herd" mentality as a result of over enthusiasm, new construction of space lags economic and market conditions. Excess new construction turns into overbuilding when new building continues during an economic and market slow down.

For example, it takes an average of two years to construct an office building, so when an office developer starts planning, gathering permits, and negotiating with contractors, the real estate market could look very strong. But, two years later as the new building comes online to occupy, the market may have collapsed. This lag creates overbuilding in the marketplace as new construction continues beyond the falling demand for new space. An example of "Lag" is clearly evident in the following chart entitled, "Real Estate Supply & Demand Cycle."

If new supply of space could be produced or withdrawn instantaneously, the market would always be in equilibrium, and there would be no cycle. But in reality, a considerable lag exists between the time demand for more space is identified and the time new space becomes available.

## Real Estate Supply & Demand Cycle

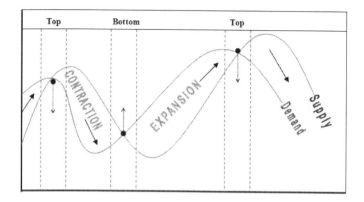

Note the "Lag" in Supply after Demand reverses course

- As Demand turns down, Supply continues up a bit longer before reversing

- As Demand turns up, Supply continues down a bit longer before reversing

In an interview with Chad Carpenter of Reven Capital, a private opportunistic and value real estate investor, he said, "I started buying notes and office buildings in '92, '93, and every deal was like 80, 90, 100% return – per year return on equity. You buy in '92, '93, '94, sell it in '95, '96 – just knocking it out of the park deals, and those returns can be made, but again, we're trying to buy a lot of deals, and we're just trying to make investors 20%."

## Timing the Real Estate Market

Timing is extremely critical when buying real estate. As Roger W. Barson said, "In selecting the soundest financial investments, the question of when to buy is far more important than what to buy." The principal rule "buy low, sell high" applies to real estate as it does to any type of investment. The best time to make a future profit is when the real estate is acquired. The ability to recognize real estate cycles gives an investor the added edge to make informed investment decisions on timing.

When the real estate market begins to recover from its contraction, it goes through a recovery period where vacant space begins to be absorbed faster than new space coming on the market, thus the beginning of the absorption cycle. A contrarian investor recognizes this supply and demand change, where demand out-paces supply, creating an opportunity to purchase real estate at the bottom of the market. As demand continues to expand from a growing economy through expanding businesses and job growth, rents, occupancies and values begin to increase.

I recently spoke with Christopher E. Lee, a leading real estate consultant to over 500 real estate companies and author on real estate cycles. I asked him where he sees the real estate cycle today. Mr. Lee said, "I believe we are now in the bottoming out period, and we are going to see some early indicators of improvement (values increasing, a pick-up in leasing activity, increased investor interest, and improving fundamentals) throughout 2010 and into 2011. By 2012, we should be out of this transition phase and into a new growth phase."

As our economy begins to recover and turn around, demand should begin to occur and create the growth real estate needs. The supply of commercial real estate has basically been in check through this cycle. Given a pick-up in demand, real estate occupancies, rental rates and values could take off because obtaining financing for new development is years off, putting downward pressure on new supply. Measuring the downside risk against the upside potential of buying investment properties beginning in 2010 and 2011, one can see the potential positive impact to investors' financial performance.

Craig Hall, a distinguished value real estate investor of over 40 years, wrote a book in 2003 entitled, *Timing the Real Estate Market: How to Buy Low and Sell High in Real Estate*. He offers this relevant case study:

In the mid-70's, during a very uncertain and difficult time in New York's history, rents and occupancy tumbled in the office market to the point the market reached bottom in late 1976. Many developers and owners of properties were washed out of the business, where new construction came to a standstill. Olympia and York, an aggressive and successful real estate company from Canada, saw this as an opportunity. They purchased several office buildings at the cycle bottom from a large New York real estate developer for $320 million with a $50 million down payment. Many people in the real estate business thought they were crazy as the market had been filled with a lot of pessimism.

They accurately realized the market had bottomed in 1976 because new construction (supply) had been greatly reduced, job growth had begun to strengthen as the economy expanded out from a recession, and pessimism was at an all time high. In less than five years, the Olympia and York purchase had appreciated in value to more than $2 billion. Buildings that had been purchased for $75 or less per square foot in some cases were renting for more than that per year.

Correctly timing the real estate market is critical to an investor's long term financial success. Investors have built and lost large fortunes in real estate as a result of the effects of real estate cycles. Think about where we are in the current real estate cycle. Are we on the precipice of the next great buying opportunity?

## Real Estate Cycles Review

Real estate cycles have a significant impact on the financial success and failure of real estate investments because of their pervasive dynamic impacts on real estate returns, risks and investment values. Because of this recognition, investors need to place increased emphasis on the identification, analysis and decision-making implications of real estate cycles.

It should be recognized that over a complete real estate cycle, most average investors guess wrong a large percentage of time because they "gallop with the herd" and follow conventional crowd wisdom. In contrast, successful investors that consistently outperform the market average are willing to follow a path contrary to that of the masses.

Thus, good timing and a degree of contrarianism are key ingredients to successful investing that achieves above-market returns over a long period of time. Investments must be bought and sold before cyclical trends are fully reflected in real estate prices and activity. An investor must be an independent thinker forecasting cycles and acting ahead of popular opinion - buying when popular opinion is still negative and most investors are trying to sell, and selling when popular opinion says the boom is on and speculative investor buying causes asset prices to increase beyond economic reason.

# Gain the Strategic Advantage
# For the Next Real Estate
# Boom Cycle

With the market meltdown over the last couple of years, where are we in the real estate cycle? Can we predict and forecast real estate cycles? I am speaking with Christopher E. Lee, CEO of CEL & Associates, a leading real estate consultant and authority on predicting real estate cycles. Chris sheds some much needed light on where we are in the real estate meltdown, uncovers methods you can use to predict real estate cycles, and reveals how to position your investments in the coming years to capitalize on the next boom cycle.

**You have written a great deal about real estate cycles. Can you describe what you've found?**

Based on over three decades of research and my experience and exposure to over 500 real estate firms, I have discovered that real estate cycles tend to follow a fairly consistent 10-year pattern. Within this 10-year period, there are four phases, or periods, of change/opportunity. The first phase is the Growth Period, the second is the Plateau Period, the third is the Crisis Period and the final phase is the Transition Period. It appears that the best time to enter the cycle is during the Transition Period, and the best time to exit is probably six to 12 months prior to the Plateau Phase peak.

Now, it is important to remember that all asset classes or markets do not begin or end a cycle at the same time. Our research indicates that the impact of global, state and regional economic and government activity (taxes, regulations, oversight, etc.) influences the length and/or severity of a real estate cycle.

Most real estate cycles, however, begin around the third year of a decade (1973, 1983, 1993, etc.) and usually end by the eighth year of the same decade (1978, 1988, 1998, etc.). The transition period occurs between the finish and the start of a new cycle and usually lasts approximately four years (1979-1982, 1989-1992, 1999-2002, etc.).

## Where do you see the real estate cycle today?

We are in the second year of the current four-year transition period (2009-2012). I believe we are now in a "bottoming out" period, and we are going to see some earlier indicators of improvement (values increasing, a pick-up in leasing activity, an increased investor interest, and improving fundamentals) throughout 2010 and into 2011. By 2012, we should be out of this transition phase and into a new growth phase.

## When do you think the next real estate boom will begin?

While it is difficult to pick a precise date for the next real estate boom, our research indicates that 2016-2018 should be a great time to be an owner of real estate. But remember, not all markets are equal, and some markets clearly will outperform others during this time.

## What sectors will drive real estate growth during the next cycle?

Our market intelligence tells us that the drivers in the next real estate cycle are likely to be green technologies, healthcare, energy and alternative energy, data storage, knowledge-centered industries, bio-tech, opportunities created by recapitalization, generational shifts and government-related industries.

## What asset types do you like the best to emerge from this growth period?

The assets likely to recover first from the crisis period and become the best leading indicators of the new growth phase will be apartments, healthcare and grocery-anchored retail. We have found in our studies that after a recession, the consumer tends to follow Abraham Maslow's Hierarchy of Needs (from a 1943 paper entitled, "A Theory of Human Motivation"). Maslow's research indicated that individuals tend to address the "basics" before they participate in forms of indulgence. Thus, food, shelter and wellness are priorities - hence, the strong likelihood that the multifamily, healthcare and grocery-anchored retail asset classes will do well. We are already seeing indicators of this in several markets today.

**What geographic markets appear to have the best opportunity for growth over, let's say, the next three to five years?**

The best geographic markets for growth over the next three to five years are likely to be 24/7 capital cities, knowledge center areas, specialty cities, string cities, government centers and gateway cities. The suburbs of the past will give way to a new urban revitalization. Over the long term, we like areas such as Northern Virginia, Boston, New York, Nashville, Raleigh, Cambridge, Houston, Seattle, Denver, Chicago and Atlanta. The best state by far is, and will probably continue to be, Texas. The best region will be the Sunbelt, while probably one of the more challenging states to conduct business will be California.

**What sectors will drive real estate growth during the next cycle?**

The primary sectors, as mentioned earlier, are going to be healthcare, seniors, technology, government-related activities, defense and security, communications, research and development, waste management, emerging technologies, alternative energy, energy in general, science, Internet-based technologies, software and programming and hardware, pharmaceuticals, and financial management. We have identified at least 50 different industries that will grow and represent tremendous future opportunity over the next 10 – 15 years.

**Christopher E. Lee**
President & CEO, CEL & Associates

Serving the needs of over 500 clients in the U.S., Canada and Europe, CEL & Associates, Inc.'s advice, forecasts, insights and predictions have made Christopher Lee a much sought after consultant for over 30 years. Chris's expertise is in such demand that he has over 7,000,000 frequent flyer miles.

Mr. Lee serves as the editor for *Strategic Advantage*, a nationwide publication received by approximately 20,000 senior executives of real estate companies. In a recent issue of *Strategic Advantage* entitled, "Real Estate Cycles - They Exist...And Are Predictable," Chris offers a complete study on real estate cycles.

Mr. Lee is a frequent contributor to national journals and a keynote speaker at conferences sponsored by national associations. Mr. Lee has co-authored a book on the Development Process for hotel facilities, and also authored a book titled, *From Good to Great to Best- in- Class, A Real Estate Leader's Guide to Optimal Performance.*

# Chapter 3

## *The Principles of Real Estate Value Investing*

*"We're buying one hotel now; we're under contract, and we're buying it for about 21% of replacement cost. It's about 11 cap rate. The old owner actually put about seven million dollars of upgrades into it. There's nothing really to do but clean it up and resurface the parking lot and reflag it, or rebrand it, and we think we're going to make about 4x multiple on equity on that deal."*

> Chad Carpenter
> Reven Capital

The principles of real estate value investing outlined in this book are built around the framework of Benjamin Graham, the grandfather of value investing. Graham's overall central theme is buying investments that are undervalued using his three simple principles:

1. Conducting Thorough Analysis
2. Preservation of Capital
3. Obtaining Attractive Yield

Ben Graham's value investing strategy focused on buying investments with the same discipline as an insurance underwriter, carefully considering the risks, rejecting potential investments that have too much uncertainty, and insisting upon a margin of safety in the event his calculation of intrinsic value was too optimistic. Graham's principles distinguish between investment versus speculation and gambling.

Ben Graham is widely recognized as the first proponent of value investing. He was an economist and professional investor who began teaching value investing in 1928 at Columbia Business School. Ben is known for his bestselling books, *Security Analysis* and *The Intelligent Investor*, which lay out his value investing principles. Warren Buffet, a Graham disciple, credits Graham for grounding him with a sound intellectual investment framework, and describes him as the second most influential person in his life after his own father.

As real estate value investors, we use Graham's framework and principles to invest in real estate assets that are based on thorough evaluation, buying below intrinsic value and generating high yielding safe returns. Real estate value investors "buy low and sell high." Growth oriented real estate investors who have the strategy of "buy high and sell higher" are not the focus of this book.

We will focus on finding and evaluating properties that can be purchased below their intrinsic value, or properties that offer, through conservative and thorough analysis, value enhancement strategies to create future value.

## Conducting Thorough Analysis

Value investors tirelessly uncover all facts pertinent to making investment decisions. No credence is given to hunches, guesses, fads, or irrational forecasting and assumptions. Worst case scenarios are always considered over best case scenarios. Value investors are looking to eliminate all future surprises and reduce any risk that could affect investment performance. They don't jump on the bandwagon; they are independent thinkers who make their own decisions based on thorough analysis.

Finding good value opportunities is difficult. So when you find an interesting value investment opportunity, do your homework. Examine the competition, the property, the market, and the viability of the business plan that's expected to capture the value.

## Preservation of Capital

Warren Buffet has two rules when making an investment. Rule No. 1: Never lose money. Rule No. 2: Never lose money. Buffet understands that nothing destroys wealth building faster than loss of capital. So, never lose money by preserving your capital.

The best way to accomplish preservation of capital is to buy real estate investments with a margin of safety. The price you pay for an investment asset must always be significantly below the appraisal value or the intrinsic value. The price you pay for an investment must support a value component where value is bought or created during the life of the investment. Also, excessive leverage offers too much risk and depreciates the notion of buying with a margin of safety.

Ben Graham writes, "A true margin of safety is one that can be demonstrated by figures, by persuasive reasoning, and by reference to a body of actual experience." Using actual historical data to support the margin of safety with factually supportive forecasting is critical to achieving preservation of capital. Anything less, and Graham views it as speculation.

The real estate crash that began in 2008 was fraught with real estate investors speculating. Investors were over paying for real estate assets using excessive leverage that led to a financial crisis of a lifetime, causing the second worst recession on record. As a result, real estate prices plummeted. Investors have routinely violated Graham's rules, and losing capital was pervasive among investors.

For over 30 years, Rance King of RK Properties has been a big believer in value creation and creating a margin of safety supported by thorough analysis. A few years ago, he purchased an 11-story vacant failed condo conversion in Ft. Lauderdale, Florida, from Bank of America. Rance says, "We ended up being one of eleven bidders and I think because we had known of this building for so long, we knew it better than anyone else, and I was willing to go hard with a bigger deposit, we got the building. It is only 150 units, but I put about $2.2 million into it – new kitchens, bathrooms, granite, new cabinets, resort-style pool, new gym, new business center, and just made it gorgeous. I raised the rents about 30%. It's been a little over a year, and we just hit 93% occupancy."

## Obtaining Attractive Returns

To achieve attractive returns, real estate investors must ensure both cash flow and equity build-up create total returns that are north of 12% in low interest rate environments and 18% plus in high interest rate conditions. To achieve these results with a margin of safety, don't pay higher prices with unattractive yields.

As a result of the great real estate crash that started in 2008, there are many favorable buying opportunities for investors to buy real estate value deals that provide both a margin of safety and an attractive yield.

### Finding Intrinsic Value

Real estate value investors believe that real estate assets have an underlying intrinsic value that can be determined by analysis and evaluation. Opportunities for profitable investments become present when the purchase price of the asset is below the underlying intrinsic value of that asset. Value investors evaluate an opportunity in an investment by understanding the relationship between value and price. Thus, the essential task of a successful real estate value investor is to determine the intrinsic value to capitalize on inefficient market mispricing.

*Replacement Cost*

In determining the intrinsic value of real estate investment assets, there are two generally accepted practices used by fundamental investors today. The first is to determine the replacement cost of the investment asset to assess a general valuation. Adjustments are then made to the general valuation for the impact of depreciation on an older asset relative to new construction. In addition, an adjustment must be made for replacement rents versus new development rents. The end result is the intrinsic value of the investment asset.

Replacement cost numbers are typically generated on rough estimates of cost per square foot suggested by development and contractor organizations. When assessing replacement cost on an investment asset, contact two or three reputable developers or contractors, familiar with your market and product type, to obtain replacement cost estimates. Make sure your estimates are an apples-to-apples comparison that include standard costs such as:

- Hard Costs (Site, building, parking)
- Soft Costs (Third party consultants, permits & fees)
- Contingency Costs
- Land Cost
- Fees (Developer, construction, profit)
- Marketing & Leasing Costs
- Financing Costs

Finding a property's intrinsic value using the replacement cost approach is used most often in the real estate industry. The current industry replacement cost for a particular market and product type gives investors a baseline for valuation purposes. For example, let's look at a typical real estate cycle.

The economy is coming out of a recession, and demand for residential and commercial real estate is increasing. The increase necessitates the need for more housing units and commercial space to accommodate the growth. A house that cost $100,000 to build and that sells to a buyer for $120,000 creates a profit of $20,000. As the economy continues to expand and grow, replacement cost may increase to $110,000 (increase in land and building costs) and selling prices may increase to $150,000, creating a $40,000 profit. As the economy overheats and demand starts to fall, fewer buyers are available to purchase, causing home prices to fall. We enter a recession and the market is flooded with homeowners and home builders trying to sell their huge inventory of homes to fewer buyers, causing home prices to fall even farther. The replacement cost of a home now drops to $90,000 (lower land prices and cheaper commodities) and selling prices have dropped to $70,000. When the economy begins to pick up again, home prices increase as the large inventory of homes for sale decreases.

The best time to be a buyer of homes is when the replacement cost to build a home is above the selling price. Buyers can buy homes lower than it cost to build a new home creating value. If a buyer bought a home for $70,000 and the replacement cost (intrinsic value) is $90,000, then the buyer has captured, at least, $20,000 of value. When the economy picks back up, home prices need to get above $90,000 (the cost to build a home) to make a profit.

The rule of thumb is to be a buyer of real estate when prices fall below replacement cost, and a builder of real estate when prices get above replacement cost. Therefore, replacement cost is the line in the sand (baseline). As a real estate value investor, you dream of the days when prices fall below replacement cost because value opportunities are everywhere.

*Present Value of Future Income – Discounted to NPV*

The other generally accepted practice to determining the intrinsic value of real estate investment assets is to find the present value of future cash flows, known as the net present value (NPV). Present value is properly calculated as the sum of current and future cash flows with each dollar of future cash flow appropriately discounted to take into account the time value of money. Future cash flows are discounted to present values using that rate of interest that the investor could earn in the next best alternative investment (opportunity cost of capital).

Forecasting change that creates assumptions in future cash flow, as a result of value creation strategies mentioned in this book, should be done conservatively, taking into account thorough market analysis.

Let's use a sample of an investor buying a property for $1,000,000 for cash that has a value creation opportunity. Our investor is able to find an alternative investment of similar risk yielding 7% (discounted present value). The property will be held for four years and then sold.

| Year | Cash Flow |
|---|---|
| Initial Investment | (1,000,000) |
| 1 | 0 |
| 2 | 50,000 |
| 3 | 60,000 |
| 4  Cash flow + Sale Proceeds | 1,800,000 |
| **Net Present Value (NPV)** | **$1,465,861** |

Our investor is able to buy a property for $1,000,000, below the intrinsic value of $1,465,861. Looks like a good value opportunity, assuming our investor forecasted reasonable and conservative forecasting assumptions. Forecasting future cash flow and the sales price should be guided and supported by factual data. Also, the discount rate should reflect market conditions. An increase in the discount yield from 7%, in the example, to 13% would reduce the NPV to $1,184,714.

The NPV calculation was done using a financial calculator. If you don't already have a financial calculator, I recommend getting one. A financial calculator will help you assess value and yields. I use an older version called the HP12C, which is still sold today. Using my HP12C, I calculated the Internal Rate of Return (IRR) to be 18% on this sample investment.

To find the most accurate intrinsic valuation, investors should determine both the replacement cost and net present value of the investment asset. These findings should be measured and assessed against each other to determine the most accurate intrinsic value of an investment asset.

**Searching for Value**

Ultimately, real estate value investors are searching for ways to find, predict or create value. Because real estate is relatively cheap in today's market climate, finding value can be as easy as buying properties below replacement cost from distressed sellers. There is a lot of low hanging fruit where opportunities exist to purchase top notch properties. For example, Michael Brennan with Brennan Investment Group recently bought a 217,000 square foot industrial building, well below replacement cost, using cheap 5% low leveraged financing that cash flows on 60% occupancy.

Other real estate investors are creating value using more advanced strategies buying existing properties and adding value by repositioning their asset using various value enhancement strategies. Take Bill Bennett of Iconic Development for example. He's buying class C multifamily properties in class A locations and repositioning them to a student tenant base getting 25% higher rents.

Michael Schwartz with Strategic Storage Trust is creating value in the storage facility space by buying storage properties in rebounding high growth markets. He's buying properties with favorable pricing and positioning his properties to take advantage of growing markets throughout the country - creating value!

All of these real estate investors have a targeted strategy they implement to purchase real estate using value investing principles. We will discuss in greater detail the most common strategies being used today.

## Top 10 Real Estate Value Investor Traits

1. Avoid the herd mentality
2. Don't invest in markets or product types they don't understand
3. Need to have competent management
4. Understand simple is better than complex
5. Avoid proposals that support easy profits or risk free offers
6. Prefer lower leveraged deals
7. Need facts not hunches
8. Prefer cash flow sooner rather than later
9. Look to pay $.50 for $1.00
10. Need to see a well thought out business plan that solves a problem

## VALUE INVESTOR PROFILE
*An Interview with Chad Carpenter*

# How to Buy and Sell Opportunistic and Value Add Deals for High Returns

Chad Carpenter is founder and chairman of Reven Capital, a private real estate equity firm. Chad has been involved with over $2 billion of opportunistic and value add real estate and generated 28% net returns to investors for 15 years on realized deals. Chad shares with us the process he goes through to buy a good deal and how he made a $4 million profit in 18 months on a value add deal.

**You're very passionate about the opportunistic and value real estate investing. In fact, it's been the real focus of your entire career. Can you give us some background on how you got started?**

Actually, I always wanted to be a developer, and I was doing brokerage, and by 1990, this thing called a "recession" came up, and I was going to start my development business, and I was asking people, "Hey, what's a recession?" I realized that's something where you don't do any development.

I was representing REO departments, selling their investment properties as their real estate advisor, and I was selling these deals, and the deals were so good. I remember one deal in particular. I sold it to a buyer, and the buyer bought it for about 30% of replacement cost, and it was a 40% cash-on-cash deal at 50% leased, and the seller provided 80% financing on the deal. So I said to myself, "Why would anybody build anything when you can buy it for 30 cents on the dollar and make that kind of return?" And a light bulb went on, kind of in my head, saying I should be buying these deals, not building them or brokering them, and that was kind of the launch of my passion to buy distressed commercial real estate and opportunistic real estate.

## Can you tell us a little bit about Reven Capital?

The business model for Reven Capital is to create an investment platform and have niche opportunistic funds in different asset classes at different times of the market. We have niche funds that range from $100 million to $250 million. Different strategies are good at different times in the market; not every strategy should be replicated all the time, if opportunity's are not there.

So the thought was to be more of the fund manager partner with operating partners in the fund and change your strategies so you've got the right strategy at the right time in the market to hopefully deliver the best superior risk-adjusted returns for investors. In the past, if you were stuck in one asset class, at some period of time that asset class is probably peaking and is not a good time to invest in that asset class. We thought the strategy was more efficient and flexible, and so far, so good.

## What types of properties that you're looking at?

We've got a couple different strategies. We're looking for hotels – three to five-star hotels across the U.S., basically all foreclosure deals or bankruptcy situations in most major markets and secondary markets. Also we have a residential strategy where we're looking for finished lots, partially finished lots, entitled land for residential projects, and broken condos in California, Arizona, and Nevada – those are our two fund strategies. We also are looking for office buildings, opportunistic office buildings and opportunistic bulk condos across the U.S. with some other partners.

## How are you sourcing properties?

We're talking to banks directly, at the executive level. We've got some investment bankers we're working with that are calling directly at the CFO level for us. We are working with brokers on the ground floor to source deals, preferably off-market deals. And we're also working with borrowers, in some cases, to recapitalize and restructure their deals, to salvage that situation and get our capital to work in that instance.

## You're looking at some hotels as well as some broken condo deals. It's the right time in the cycle for those opportunities?

Yes, absolutely. If you take the trough and the peak, our view of the real estate world is the residential asset class was the first asset class off the peak. Looking back in hindsight now and seeing what happened, subprime clearly pulled residential down a year or even two years potentially ahead of commercial real estate.

But hospitality, I think, literally, when Lehman Brothers went upside down in September of 2008, immediately everybody panicked and stopped traveling. Leisure travel shut down; business travel shut down; and hotels, unfortunately, got crushed. And so cash flows in hotels immediately dropped, and they just got walloped. And it left a lot of hotel owners with no cash flow to cover their debt service. And now, after about a year, we're seeing just a Tsunami of foreclosures. There are so many hotels in foreclosure right now that we can't even keep up with the deal flow. There's so much deal flow, which is fantastic, and we're buying a few right now.

## What are your plans with the ones that you're looking to buy?

Actually, we're buying one hotel now; we're under contract, and we're buying it for about 21% of replacement cost. It's about an 11 cap rate. The old owner actually put about seven million dollars of upgrades into it. There's nothing, really, to do but clean it up and resurface the parking lot and reflag it, or rebrand it, and we think we're going to make about 4x multiple on equity on that deal. And so we're very excited about that deal. That's a deal we're under contract on now. That's actually in San Diego, so even in San Diego, you can get a great deal.

**How long a hold are you looking for to get your 4x?**

This particular deal the business plan is to hold it for five years, based on our assumptions, but normally opportunistic real estate, you're anywhere from two to five years. If you have an empty office building, you buy it for $40.00 a foot when it cost $250.00 to build and then you lease it up. As soon as you get it leased, you've added the value, so you sell it. So you could do that in a year. I've sold deals in nine months to two and a half years. As soon as you fill them, you sell them. Hotels are a little different; you're subject to somewhat of a market recovery play. It's not like an office building where it's empty and you sign one big lease and you're done.

**Can you give us an example of a value-add deal you've done that kind of exemplifies what you've talked about?**

I bought three office buildings in Phoenix from an opportunity fund on the East Coast. I paid about $35 million for them, and I put about 11 million of equity down. They were all less than 50% leased, and basically, over an average of two and a half years, I was able to lease them up to over 90% and sold them out for about $72 million. We turned $11 million dollars into a significant profit for our investors. And that's an example of opportunistic or value-add, where you fill the buildings; you increase the revenues, increase the net operating income, and enhance the value.

**What are three or four must-have deal points for you that you have to have in your deal that are great value opportunities that you're really looking for as part of your criteria?**

We write a lot of offers on deals. There was this one medical office building I chased – and this is years ago, in the last downturn. It was just a small deal, but the story's fantastic:

The insurance company foreclosed on a medical office building in San Diego, actually, and it was a $6.5 million dollar loan, and the tenants moved out. It was about 20% leased, so they put this property on the market with a good broker in town for six and a half million because they wanted their loan paid back.

There were no offers on it, so I underwrote it and did what I did: what can I sell it for, what is it going to cost me to get there, what can I pay for it, what's the cost of my equity? I can't pay more than a million five, million six for this thing. So I wrote an offer for a million five. Lots of buyers don't want to offend brokers and sellers, but my attitude is, well, that's all I can pay because that's what it costs to turn it around. I don't have a problem submitting an offer to the broker.

So I submitted the offer. I offended the broker, I offended the seller with my million five offer, and I said, "Well, would you buy it for a million five?" And they said, "Oh, absolutely, we'd buy it for a million five." So I said, "It's a good offer, right?" "No, no, it's a bad offer." So literally a year goes by, and the same property came out with a new flyer – price reduction $4.5 million.

I looked at it again, re-ran the numbers. I think I can pay a million six, million seven, but I said, "Nah, I'll write a million five." I submitted the offer back at a million five. I get the same thanks, but no thanks, we're not interested.

A year later, a new flyer comes out for 2.9; they're asking $2.9 million. So I didn't even write a new offer; I just grabbed the old one that was a year old, and I said, "Here. Remember this offer – this year-old one for a million five? Let's do the deal?" Long story short, I bought it for a million seven, leased it up in 18 months, and sold it for $5.4 million.

**What kinds of returns are you looking for over a typical holding period of, let's say, two to five years?**

Our goal is to net investors 20% per year, and then make some money for ourselves, so I'd say a 25% and up project level return is our minimum on deal flow. So if you can get better, fantastic, which I have done a lot better in the last downturn.

I started buying notes and office buildings in '92, '93, and every deal was like 80, 90, 100% return per year return on equity. You buy in '92, '93, '94, sell it in '95, '96 – just knocking out of the park deals, and those returns can be made, but again, we're trying to buy a lot of deals, and we're just trying to make investors 20%.

## What about cash flow? Will the deals throw off cash flow in the first?

It depends on what you buy. It depends what asset class you buy. The hotels we're focused on, we're looking to buy hotels at least a 10 cap rate on trailing 12 months (operating numbers). So to the extent we're buying that, we'll be cash flowing day one on the assumption that it's not going to get worse, so we'll have consistent cash flow.

On office buildings and retail buildings, most of the stuff we buy will have no cash flow or even negative NOI because if you're half-leased, and those assets are so capital-intensive with TI's and commissions and fixing capital improvements, roofs, chillers, lobbies, bathrooms, etc. The cash flow's minor compared to the amount of money you've got to put back into the asset to turn it around. So with office and retail, we're not really focused on cash flow, but I think from the hotel aspect, there will be some good cash flow.

## Chad Carpenter
Founder, Reven Capital

Chad is Founder and Chairman of Reven Capital, a private real estate equity firm that co-sponsors opportunistic and value add real estate with partners who can execute a niche strategy within the partner's expertise.

Chad has been involved with over $2 billion of opportunistic and value add real estate and generated 28% net returns to investors for 15 years on realized deals.

In 2005, Mr. Carpenter was selected as one of Real Estate Southern California's "40 Under 40." In 2007, he was a finalist for the Ernst & Young Entrepreneur Of The Year® Award in San Diego and was also chosen as one of the "20 Rising Stars of Real Estate" globally by Institutional Investor News.

# Chapter **4**

## *Approaches to Creating Value*

*"The City Parkway deal, which is a 450,000 square foot office project, is 20% leased. I bought it all cash so it is cash flowing. I actually made a distribution to my partners on a 20% leased building."*

Mike Jenkins
The Abbey Company

Creating value can be as simple as buying a property that's in great condition and in a great location in a rebounding and growing community. But, creating value can also demand very specialized expertise and knowledge, like buying an underutilized property and re-developing the property into another completely different use. Over the last century, the most used approaches to creating value have been somewhere in middle, where some expertise is required.

We will look at two approaches to creating value that require different levels of expertise and investment horizons. The first approach is "forced appreciation opportunities" where value investors actively engage in strategies to create value in the short term. Investors search for investment opportunities where they can use their expertise and knowledge to force value creation through hands-on activities. The second approach is "emerging growth opportunities" where value investors uncover external economic or market activities that are expected to lead to growing opportunities in the long term. Both approaches involve the process of value creation on investments, whether over the short term or long term.

## Forced Appreciation Opportunities

Real estate value investors that use the forced appreciation approach like to take control of their investments, not waiting for outside occurrences to happen. The old saying, "If it's to be, it's up to me," is a hands-on approach many investors use to create their own appreciation. These types of investors can create large returns through their expertise, hard work, market intelligence, shrewd observations, relationships and unique strategies.

Back in the early 90's, I bought a tired 20-unit apartment building in Phoenix from an inexperienced investor. I bought the property well below the market value in a short sale with the seller and his lender. I gave the property a nice swift kick in the butt with new management and some renovations, raised the rents over a four year period and sold a turn-key, fully occupied property to another investor for a nice profit. My investors and I made 10 times our investment in four short years.

Looking back now, it's easy to see the great profit potential. But, what's hard to see is all the hard work and hassles that accompanied this property. Was it worth it? Heck yes. Without my effort and hands-on work, the profit may never have happened. Most forced appreciation deals can be quite active and hands-on.

### All Properties are Not Fixers

There are many ways to create value through forced appreciation that do not involve fixing properties. Generally, most people believe that to create value you need to get dirty by renovating properties. Not true. Savvy real estate investors that have good negotiating skills, combined with being at the right place at the right time, can buy properties or notes at significant discounts, especially in today's real estate environment.

For example, real estate value investor, The Magellan Group, purchased a $45M note for $32.2M, a 28.4% discount on a 100% leased, 531,000 sq. ft. industrial building. The as-is appraisal was $49,500,000, creating a significant value creation for The Magellan Group and a very safe loan for Mesa West Capital.

Properties are available to buy with value creation opportunities that are in great condition. With the distressed debt market, many top properties have been subjected to mortgage defaults. Shrewd investors either buy the notes at a discount or buy the property through a short sale.

## Research Leads to Making Great Deals

All value creation opportunities are based on the foundation of research. Good ideas are supported by research. Medical breakthroughs are founded on good research. Technological advances are based on research. Research is the very essence to finding and proving value creation opportunities are viable. Without studying and researching, value investors are stuck with guesswork, speculation, and hunches that may lead to poor investments. It's like buying your home over the internet without ever seeing it - simply baseless.

It's amazing the number of investors that buy real estate without researching their investments. Peter Lynch, the superstar money manager, said, "Know what you're investing in and why." To find the answer to WHY you are investing in a deal, you need to investigate and research your reasoning.

Value investors that invest in niche tenant bases need to research to find the best tenant base to target. Value investors that are planning to reposition a property need to research to find out who they're repositioning it to. Ivan Boesky said in the *Wall Street Journal* back in 1987, "My advice to investors is the same that I give to young investors in my classes. Devote the same earnest attention to investing that $50,000 as you devoted to earning it."

## Entrepreneurial and Enterprising Spirit

Forced appreciation opportunities require entrepreneurial foresight when buying real estate deals to plan and budget the value creation. First, an investor needs to see the value potential a property might contain.  Many times, the real key to being a real estate value investor is seeing value or missed opportunities that others don't see.

Are there things you can add to a property that will increase rents? Does the property need better management? Is the property serving the highest and best use tenant profile to get the highest rents? Can you re-design space to generate more revenues? Are there services, features or amenities that you can add to generate higher revenues?

Once you've found ways to create value, next you must create a well thought out business plan that lays out your value creation vision. The essence of your plan should very pointedly spell out how you are going to create value and make money with the property.  This plan will be used to execute your plan, as well as help you raise debt and equity funds.

Finally, you will need to sell your plan to potential stakeholders.  If you have found a rock solid deal with lots of value creation opportunities, getting buy-in from potential partners will be easy.  But in the end, the ability to see value in a deal and be able to communicate the value you see will be critical. Let your entrepreneurial and enterprising spirit shine.

I raised $10 million from one investment fund to partner with me to buy a three property portfolio of multifamily properties in the Phoenix area.  The value creation opportunity was to reposition the assets toward the Hispanic theme tenant base.  I presented a detailed business plan that clearly supported the underserved niche opportunity to my investor. When we met in Phoenix to see the properties, I was able to factually communicate the value creation opportunity.  We eventually partnered to buy the properties. Be entrepreneurial with your thinking.  Find better ways to do things that create value, and the support from stakeholders will be there for you.

## Emerging Growth Opportunities

Jim Cramer of "Mad Money" says, "There is always a bull market somewhere." Even when the stock market is in a bear market and going down, Jim Cramer finds buying opportunities in stocks that are in a bull market going up. The real estate market is made up of smaller submarkets located throughout the world. Real estate prices may be going down in Las Vegas, Nevada, but they're going up in Sydney, Australia. There is always somewhere to find emerging growth opportunities to create value.

Earlier, we were talking about the importance of research. The only way you're going to find emerging growth opportunities is through research. Emerging growth opportunities aren't yelling out saying, "Over here!" Part of your research should include watching the big whale investors. What are they doing and why? At the very minimum, find out what they're doing so that it gives you something to research to confirm their strategy. One of the best places to learn about the leading real estate value investors is to go to http://www.HaskellValueRealEstateInvestor.com and read the detailed interviews.

## Search For Undervalued Communities

Can you uncover the next Orange County, California? Until 1950, Orange County was a heavy agricultural area with acres of orange trees and strawberry fields. By the mid-1950s, Orange County's farms were being replaced by tract housing faster than any other community in the United States. Existing cities began annexing territory in every direction, and new cities incorporated almost every year.

Between 1953 and 1962, Buena Park, Costa Mesa, La Palma, Garden Grove, Cypress, Westminster, Fountain Valley, Los Alamitos, San Juan Capistrano, and Villa Park all voted to incorporate. In 1963, the county population topped one million. Tourism, manufacturing, and the service industry began to dominate the local economy. The opening of Disneyland in 1955 made Orange County an international tourist destination. By 1980, the population had doubled in size to over 2 million people in just 20 years time. This undervalued community became a real estate bonanza for investors.

There are many undervalued communities around the world where real estate value investors can find emerging growth opportunities. Could Brazil be the next Orange County? Bloomberg wrote about Sam Zell, famous value investor, in a May, 2010 article, "Zell's Firm Raising $500 Million for Brazil Property":

> "Billionaire investor Sam Zell's Equity International is seeking to raise about $500 million to step up investment in Brazilian real estate, betting interest rate increases will fail to stem demand as the economy grows at the fastest pace in two decades. The firm will invest as much as two-thirds of the money in Brazilian companies tied to the residential and commercial property industries and the rest in other countries outside the U.S.," Chief Executive Officer, Gary Garrabrant said. The new funds will bring the Chicago-based company's total invested capital to about $2 billion.
>
> "Our enthusiasm for Brazil could not be higher," Garrabrant, who co-founded Equity International with Zell in 1999, said in a May 18 interview in Sao Paulo. "You've got this local demand that's unparalleled."
>
> "Rising incomes among Brazil's burgeoning middle class will ensure that a cycle of rate increases won't suppress housing demand," Garrabrant, 53, said. The economy will grow 6.3 percent this year, according to a central bank survey published this week. Brazilians' average monthly income has risen close to 40 percent in the past five years 1,400 reais, according to the census bureau.

You don't need to fly across the world to find emerging market opportunities; they're right in your back yard. Research your local market and look for the following clues:

- What part of town has the highest job growth?
- What part of town is experiencing well above average population growth?

- Speak with local realtors to find out popular spots.
- Are there any new industries emerging with expected growth?
- Where are the best schools?
- Is government growing anywhere?

## Discovering Rebounding Growth Markets

Many high flying, high growth markets tend to have more severe real estate boom and bust cycles. Markets like Las Vegas, Phoenix, Atlanta and others tend to experience rapid growth from high population and job growth, causing real estate construction to overbuild and create a glut of space. This leads to a bust in the real estate market leading to foreclosures and severe pricing reductions. As these markets begin to gain strength from supply of empty space being absorbed, job growth and population growth will again propel these markets.

Real estate value investors are presented with inefficient markets when the prices drop below rising strong fundamentals.

## Find Inefficient Markets

Market forces drive real estate prices higher or lower than intrinsic values. Emerging growth opportunities exist by researching and understanding mispriced real estate because of inefficient market pricing. Inefficiency means that certain players continue to have preferred access to information and expertise that allow them to capitalize upon these inefficiencies.

Everything boils down to supply and demand dynamics. Where can you find expected demand real estate needs? If supply for the demand is low, then an inefficient market exists because real estate prices are undervalued.

## You Are a Value Creator

Here's how I want you to look at yourself. You are a value creator. Your sole focus as a real estate value investor is to hunt down, uncover and find value creation opportunities for you and your investors. Find opportunities where you can use one of many strategies to create value on your real estate investments.

As Warren Buffet said, "Rule No. 1 is to not lose money." Find properties that offer a margin of safety, properties where you can purchase them below their intrinsic value to create a margin of safety so that you don't violate Rule No. 1. Once you find an undervalued property, conduct thorough research that supports and proves that you have found a value investment. Then, execute a value creation strategy with your investment that generates attractive returns.

In the next chapter, we will talk about strategies you can use to create value. What are you again? You are a value creator.

# How to Make Money Buying Opportunistic and Value Add Commercial Real Estate

Mike Jenkins is Chief Investment Officer of The Abbey Company, a value add real estate investment company. Mike uncovers the things real estate investors must consider when buying opportunistic and value add deals to best assess risk and reward. Mike shares many examples and stories of deals both from a transactional and operational perspective on things value real estate investors should be doing to be successful.

**Tell us about the Abbey Company**.

The Abbey Company is a fully integrated commercial real estate firm that was started in 1991, and has been in business primarily in Southern California. We're a firm that got started on the value-added concept in buying assets that were undermanaged and underperforming relative to what we thought they could achieve.

So we start by looking at the physical plant, looking primarily at the things that you can do on a cosmetic basis to make it more marketable, achieve higher rents, and retain tenants on a longer-term basis. We also look at the need for buildings that we acquire, which are typically older – I'd say class B or class B+ buildings. They have a lot of physical obsolescence that starts to develop by then in office buildings -elevators, HVAC's - and certainly in industrial buildings - HVAC's and roofs are things that need to be managed properly in order to extend their life and get more utility out of them.

A lot of deals we've done recently are more driven by the opportunity to buy on a price-per-pound basis. So we're buying into scenarios where you have substantial vacancy in markets that have substantial vacancy.

**The Abbey Company's undergoing a portfolio expansion to capitalize on the distressed market. Tell us how you plan to execute that.**

We have a joint venture with institutional partners now, who are interested in taking advantage, if you will, of the distress in the market. So we've been actively looking for and soliciting deals that involve distressed notes from lenders, and to some degree, directly with owners.

So we create or monitor a list of assets that are under distress, and we work with the lenders to try to determine if they are interested in us discussing with them a buy-out over that note. Sometimes they're not interested in direct negotiation, if they're going to be selling that note through an intermediary like Easton, or one of the brokers, then we want to make sure that they're aware of our interest. We're backed up by a financial partner who's got 20 million dollars in assets, and so we are able to step up and buy all cash today, which is sort of one of the keys, I think, to being a player in today's market.

**How are you finding deals?**

We are very good at tracking. We work with the broker community and track submissions. Every submission we get is booked and logged, and so we have a history. It goes back 20 years of submissions. Every one of the submissions we've got is logged and tracked, so when a submission comes in and we make an offer, quite often, we're not the buyer. But quite often, there is no buyer. And so the big trick is - I have a guy whose job is the tickler file. He goes back every six months and reviews submissions we've done six months ago, and follows up with the broker, and says, "What happened?"

So a lot of the way our submission process works is to look at the product that comes here; put our offer in so our name's out there. And we compete on everything that comes in there. We know sometimes we're not going to be the buyer, but we want to let the broker know that we're aware of the asset. And then we do a follow-up, a tickler file, and some assets take – believe it or not – two or three years later; we end up owning these things because we've tracked. We keep track of what's happened to that tenant. If the tenant's stayed or moved, we know now's the opportunity to come back and refresh that deal and see if we can make something work for both of us.

So with that file index, if you will, which is tremendous, and it's all tied to an ACT database program so we can pull up any address – any property, we can tell you what it was sold for, what it was listed for.

**Are there certain assets that you like better, based on the distressed market?**

We're a multi-tenant entity – a multi-tenant property company. We like tenants – we like assets that have a substantial number of staying tenants. We don't like to buy big, single-tenant buildings or buildings that are dependent on one tenant. The results, of course, we saw in the last year, of Ameriquest moving out and 80% of the building going empty overnight. So what we focus on is multi-tenant product.

We think, over the long run, because we have our own management team and we can deal with the tenants, a small tenant to us – a 1,500 square foot tenant - is not a problem. You know, that's bread and butter for us. So we'll focus on suburban offices. We'll focus on flex industrial. We don't know our way around the downtown office markets because you tend to deal there with a few landlords that control all the major tenants, and that's more of a collusion situation we think, so in the suburban market, smaller tenants, it's really a matter of how well you treat them. They usually aren't going to move to another building; it's too expensive for the small guy, and if you're doing a good job of managing the building and staying competitive, you can keep those tenants.

**You're paying cash for your deals, and in your underwriting, when do you see a deal starting to cash flow, become positive NOI?**

Well, there are two kinds of deals. The dichotomy is the deals we did – the City Parkway deal, which is a 450,000 square foot office project – it's 20% leased. When you say "cash flowing," you have to understand, I bought it all cash. So it is cash flowing. I actually made a distribution to my partners on a 20% leased building. The first thing I did, I had two towers; one just had a 10-story tower with one tenant in it. The former landlord was running the HVAC 24 hours a day and left the lights on. I just went in and shut the lights off, put an energy management system in, and shut down the HVAC and moved the tenant into the other tower, and I saved $100,000 a month in running that building. So I was 20% leased, and I'm distributing cash, so it's kind of like, I've got cash flow. I've got no debt, and I have very low operating costs now, and very efficient operating management. I've got one tower that's pretty full, and one building that's kind of empty. So I really am running it on 50% of what you would.

Secondly, I got a tremendous break on the property taxes when I bought the building for what I did. The taxes went 50% of what the former landlord paid. They should have gone 30% of what the former landlord paid. I'm still appealing on taxes, but obviously, you get a big tax break. All of which passes through to the tenants, by the way, through the CAM charges. And so, all of a sudden, I've got a very competitive building. I've got a building now that I can rent for 20 cents under the market to start with, and I've got CAM charges that are half of what any other building would have.

Now, nobody's going to be cheaper than me. The market's picked up now, so this building wouldn't sell for what I bought it for, but the idea is, you know, we expected other foreclosures in the market. We expect other people to be able to buy these things at a discount. We didn't think that – this deal was the perfect storm.

We had a distressed lender who wanted to get out of the market, who wanted to go back to Tokyo. We had a distressed owner – substantially distressed owner in McGuire Properties. And we had the most distressed market – Central Orange County – center of the subprime mortgage company's implosion in our market. So there weren't any saving factors, other than this is a great location; the asset right next to Anaheim Stadium had been 90 plus percent leased all its life. It was built by MetLife and Tishman back in the '70s. It's performed because of its location. It's great – right at I-5 and 22 FWY, and 57 FWY coming in. You can't find a better location. So the building has got everything going for it in terms of location, and it's been maintained relatively well.

### Tell us how this office deal compares to the flex industrial deal you just bought?

It's a flex industrial building. It was 97% leased. I also bought it all cash, so obviously, my cash flow is substantial. I bought that based more on seller circumstances. This was the perfect storm where it was distressed. This was really more a matter of a seller who had tried to sell other assets because of redemption requirements. They wanted to get some cash back into the company, into the fund that owned these things, and they weren't successful and didn't want to sell at heavy discount on the other assets. So they took an asset they'd owned for 15 years that's performed very well, and obviously sold it in a bad market, so we got a great deal because of their timing and their need to raise cash. It was really the seller – nothing about the real estate there.

I almost can't do anything to make this building and property more successful than it is. At 97% leased, there's not a lot I can bring to the table. Now, we're taking one tenant actually out of the building – they have a lease rolling over at the end of this year, and we told them they can't stay because they're over-parked, and we think that that's contributing, maybe, to some undesirability this is a tenant who had grown over 15 years, while the previous owner owned it, and was a small tenant, and now has 30,000 square feet where they've got six or seven to one parking in an industrial park that's parked less than two to one.

Fortunately, the other tenants are more industrial and hardly have any parking, but this one tenant was taking up all of it. So we had one vacancy, and nobody could figure out why the one vacancy was not leasing, and the reason there's one vacancy is there's no place to park. So we've asked this other tenant to vacate, which they will be doing, and we've put the space back on the market for more appropriate industrial types of uses. So that's kind of one thing we think we're going to do that'll actually get the building up to 100% occupancy.

**You've got two different types of deals:  the Cerritos Corporate Center and the City Parkway.  What are three or four core principles that you look for in a deal?**

Utility.  And that's a whole lot of things, in terms of does the space lay out properly for the type of uses that you envision?  We don't want to get into situations where we've got poor architectural design, we've got poor floor plan design.

We find that parking is the number one critical thing to getting a building from 70% leased to 95% leased.  If you don't have parking, you can't work the deal.  I mean three and a half to one parking for a full building is not enough.  Four to one parking is probably the minimum we'd have – if we expected to get the building fully leased.

When we bought City Parkway, we were approached by four or five tenants that wanted high parking ratios.  One was a medical provider – a dental provider, and one was a consolidator – a debt deal, consolidate and modifier.  They all wanted six, seven, eight to one parking, and we just said, no; we're not going to do it because the impact on leasing the balance of the building would have been affected.  So utility is going to be the number one criteria.

Location to us is important in two aspects:  one is that we think location is something that you should be able to immediately identify.  It's something that's got visibility and presence - curb appeal, if you will, like this building has when you drive up to it. But also, location to us is a matter of where do we own buildings in the area? Because from our point of view, we'll know the market better if we own something a mile away, and our leasing guys have been in the building and have worked this deal. We get a little more aggressive because we feel we have a lot more market insight.

What else would be important to me? I think there is a cut-off point with certain assets like age of the building, things that you just feel, at some point, you want to get out of this building at some point down the future. So I'll buy a 20-year-old building, but I probably won't buy a 30-year-old building because I figure it's going to be a 40-year-old building when I get to that point where I want to exit.

## Are there certain types of value-add components, strategies that you implement on-site that are unique or different?

First thing we look at with our engineers is how the energy management systems operate and function, and are they in a controlled environment. Do you have the ability to computerize and control when the HVACs are on and off and the lighting? They're not programmed properly, and so you end up with kind of really funky stuff where you have some parts of the building getting colder than they should be, and other parts getting hotter than they should be, and people aren't monitoring. You get into older systems in a building.

We look, first of all, at energy because the biggest savings I could pull down in a building, bottom line, are property taxes and utilities. I can save money on janitorial, and I can save money on supplies, but it's never going to be significant. Utilities and property taxes are where the big money goes.

Second of all, you've got to make sure that you are reading your leases and imposing on your tenants for after-hour uses. That's the biggest place we find found money is when we go in and read the leases and make sure that we enforce the provisions of the lease that say after-hour use gets billed out at a certain rate because quite often, tenants don't pay, and landlords don't remember. Landlords can forget to bill out for that kind of use, and we make sure that we're watching and carefully monitoring our reimbursables. And CAM charges, obviously.

You want to make sure that you're appropriately passing through everything you can, and in some cases, the leases, when you get into buildings that you don't have your standard form of lease, you're looking at a lot of modifications and amendments and changes. Over time, people forget how all of those things work. Sometimes you're overbilling the tenants; sometimes you're under-billing the tenant based on what the lease actually says.

## Mike Jenkins
CIO, The Abbey Company

Mike Jenkins is Chief Investment Officer of The Abbey Company, headquartered in Long Beach, California. The Abbey Company is a privately-held real estate investment and management firm founded in 1990 by Donald G. Abbey to acquire and manage value-added real estate investments with a current portfolio of over 50 properties encompassing in excess of 5.0 million square feet.

Mike Jenkins has over 35 years of executive entrepreneurial and corporate real estate experience working with institutional lenders and equity investors such as the Goldman Sachs, The Irvine Company, Cushman Wakefield, Dilingham Corporation, and The Shidler Group.

# Chapter 5

## *Real Estate Value Investment Strategies*

*"We were able to acquire this building at about 25% of what it takes to build it today. It was one of the lowest prices we've ever seen in O'Hare in 30 years, and it had income in place at 58% leased; income that could service the debt and also pay a dividend on our equity, with 42% more of the space to lease."*

*Michael Brennan*
*Brennan Investment Group*

We are at a fantastic time in the real estate cycle to be executing real estate value investment strategies. It's time to get off the sidelines and get in the game. While cash flow is important to an investment, the real big kahuna, that pulls the heavy weight to making money in the value investing space, is equity build-up. We are value creators. We take undervalued real estate assets and find entrepreneurial ways to make money - real money, sometimes in a very short period of time. With property values drastically down in many markets across the country, it's time to capitalize on this amazing "once in a lifetime" buying opportunity.

Through research and analysis, we can uncover value creation opportunities by identifying inefficient markets. Where have prices fallen so much below their intrinsic value that offer great value creation opportunities? Once you have uncovered a value opportunity where you can create value, you will use one of the many strategies outlined in this chapter and the next chapter.

Some strategies are easier to use while others are more advanced. Some strategies are better used early in the real estate cycle recovery while others may be better to use well into the growth period of a real estate cycle. Mix two or three strategies together and really boost the profit potential of your deal.

## Strategy #1
## Buy Real Estate Below Replacement Cost

With the deleveraging of personal and business balance sheets over the last few years coupled with the real estate market bottoming out, many opportunities exist to buy real estate assets below the cost to build similar types of buildings. Many active value investors are using this strategy.

Gary Sabin, CEO of Excel Trust, a large retail REIT that purchased more than 23 properties with total asset value close to $500 million in 2010, is focusing on buying retail properties throughout many parts of the country with the strategy of buying assets below replacement cost. He calls this the "low hanging fruit." Gary's strategy is to first buy below replacement cost shopping centers that are in great condition, in great locations, because these types of properties are the easiest to buy.

Next, as valuations increase, Gary plans to transition into other value strategies where more hands-on forced appreciation efforts will be required. This strategy involves buying great assets well below replacement cost and waiting for the new development cycle to begin. As the new development cycle begins, property valuations increase and snap back to replacement cost and continue to increase as things improve. Value investors executing this strategy enjoy cash flow during the holding period and capitalize on the value creation as things improve.

Also, some value investors take a shorter term viewpoint. They buy properties at such a discount and resell them within a very short time period, some of them within hours. Although this is not a popular strategy, it is happening in the market. When using this strategy, you must have a good handle on current property valuations and the cost of replacement. Also, it's critical to have a very good understanding of your local market and its current position in the real estate cycle.

## Case Study

*Brennan Investment Group purchased an industrial building with the strategy of buying below replacement cost and holding the property for cash flow and waiting for values to recover.*

**Subject:** *Prospect Industrial Center, 217,529 square feet on an 8.28 acre site*

**Property Description:** *Built in 1987, two multi-tenant light industrial warehouses located 2 miles north of O'Hare International Airport*

**Class & Occupancy:** *B Class Property, 59% leased to 7 tenants*

**Purchase Price:** *$3,525,000*

**Rehab Cost:** *$1,275,000*

**Cap Rate/Financing/Lev. %:** *9.15% going in Cap Rate on 59% occupancy (16% stabilized cap rate)*

*$3,400,000 Senior Loan (70.8% to total project cost)*

*$1,400,000 Investor Cash*

**Value Strategy / Opportunity:** *Brennan Investment Group saw an opportunity to acquire this functional property located in the O'Hare submarket, one of the Chicago area's strongest and most stable sectors, at a significant discount to replacement cost. The property was acquired at a 9.15% cap rate, generating sufficient income to both cover debt service and realize in excess of a 10% cash-on-cash return.*

*Principal Global Investors, a knowledgeable and capable seller, sought to sell this tenant and capital improvement intensive asset in a quick and expeditious manner. Brennan saw this as an opportunity to utilize its on-site leasing and management expertise to create value in an asset overlooked by larger real estate institutions.*

*Brennan Investment Group closed on the deal in the middle of October of 2010. At a $3.525 million purchase price, or $16.20/SF 21% of replacement cost, this transaction represents the lowest comparative property on record in almost 30 years in the O'Hare market. The company believes that through active* *management and aggressive leasing efforts, they may be able to restore the property to its former market value of between $9 million and $11 million.*

*This smaller transaction is emblematic of one of the company's strategies, acquiring one-off properties in major markets and aggregating them into a larger pool to eventually be sold either as a portfolio or merged into a public company.*

## Strategy #2
## Buy Lower Class Properties and Reposition Them to Higher Class Properties

This strategy involves finding lower class properties in good neighborhoods, upgrading them with more features, amenities and services, and then repositioning to a high quality tenant who will pay higher rents. Markets that are in transition provide good hunting grounds for these types of deals. Also, older well established markets that have of nice mix of older and newer properties are good candidates for upgrading and repositioning. Value investors can find class C properties and reposition them to class B, or they can find class B properties and reposition them to class A. Pick a niche and specialize in that niche.

For example, some value investors look for class C properties in class B locations. Older class C properties are outdated and need to be upgraded to meet the new needs of consumer and business demands. These value investors will spend capital funds to upgrade the properties from class C to class B, and therefore, will be able to charge higher rents. The reposition allows for value creation both from the increase in rental income and by the lowering of the capitalization rate.

Value investors who execute this strategy must thoroughly research their local market, economy and other competing properties. When buying a property to reposition, it's critical to determine who that new tenant is going to be. Once the new tenant is determined, a remodel program can be rolled out that meets the needs of the new tenant. Value investors need to determine the new tenant first and then remodel the property around their demands so that maximum rental growth is achieved.

## Case Study

*The Bascom Group purchased an REO from a lender with a strategy of upgrading the property from class C to a class B in a class B neighborhood. In addition, the Bascom Group bought the property so much below replacement cost that they were able to execute two value creation strategies on this property.*

**Subject:** *Maples at Crestwood, 300 Units*
*1327 West Ave 84th, Denver, CO 80260*
**Property Description:** *Built in 1973, the community is spread over 11.09 acres creating a comfortable density level (27.23 units/ac). Maples has the only townhome floor plan in the competitive set consisting of 13% studios, 52% one-bedroom and 34% two-bedroom units with an average size of 748 sf.*
**Class & Occupancy**: *Class C, 65% current physical occupancy*
**Purchase Price:** *$8,300,000*
**Rehab Cost:** *$3,885,000*
**Cap Rate/Financing/Lev. %:** *The leverage was 70% of total cost.*

**Value strategy / Opportunity:** *The property was purchased through an off-market foreclosure at a significant 77% discount to replacement cost. During the foreclosure process, the income restriction was terminated and the property can now be operated as a full market-rate apartment community. Value add strategy includes extensive renovations with added amenities and a police substation, new institutional quality management, a decrease in operating expenses, bringing rents to market rates, and increasing occupancy. The property was repositioned to a class B property with sizeable rent increase from the reposition and the elimination of rent restrictions.*

## Strategy #3
## Buy and Revitalize Underperforming Properties

Many properties are mismanaged and not performing up to market standards. This strategy involves finding properties that are suffering from poor management, low rents, high vacancy, deferred maintenance, and have struggling property owners.

Let's face it; many property owners get into the real estate game failing to realize the property they own is a business. Investment properties need to be run like a business and not an investment. The strategy for value investors is to capitalize on property owners and managers that aren't very good at running their business and injecting quality management and the needed financial resources to better operate the property. By doing so, value investors are able to create value on these types of properties, which translates into higher generating revenues and higher value.

Make sure you have a top notch management company operating your properties. 70% of the success of a property is because of good day-to-day property management. Being a landlord has its challenges so finding good and reliable property management will be important.

Also, the cost to turnaround an underperforming property can be higher than you expect. Make sure you have a conservative operating and renovation budget. The three biggest costs to budget safely for are vacancy, concessions and construction costs. My property turnaround costs always seem to cost more than I plan. Now, I add an extra 20% to my capital reserves budget. Make sure you have enough funds to complete the job correctly.

Finally, turnaround properties require aggressive marketing to attract new tenants. Hiring proven marketing specialists will be critical to your success to fill up your property. Don't be cheap when hiring good marketing people. Paying a little extra for marketing early in the process will be far cheaper than the alternative.

## Case Study

*The Conti Organization purchased a run-down apartment building from a lender with the strategy of injecting new management and marketing to turnaround the underperforming property.*

**Subject:** *Huntington Apartments*
*5700 Boca Raton Blvd, Fort Worth, Texas 76112*
**Property Description:** *Multi-family apartments; 208 Units, 9.5 Acres, 417,305 sq ft, built in 1981*
**Class & Occupancy**: *Class B, 94% Occupied*
**Purchase Price:** *$3,100,000*
**Rehab Cost:** *none*
**Cap Rate/Financing/Lev. %:** *All cash purchase for $14,900/unit*

**Value strategy / Opportunity:** *Bank owned apartment building was offered at $4,290,000 with a final purchase of $3,100,000. During the period the bank owned the property, they spent over $700,000 in improvements, leaving this property in "rent-ready" condition. Ultimately, the property only needed a better marketing/advertising campaign.*

*Upon takeover, a 2 step marketing campaign was implemented. Step one included adding office support, an office theme, banners, balloons, a tenant referral program, hiring a locater service, and distributing flyers in the area. The result was an increase in occupancy from 64% to 82% in less than 45 days.*

*For Step 2 focused on property functions, parties, blood drives, and instilling an active family community lifestyle to the property. The result was an additional increase in occupancy from 82% to 94.3% in less than 39 days.*

*Upon completion of the 84 day marketing campaign, the property was appraised at $5,500,000, a $2.4 million value add and a 77% return on equity in less than a year.*

## Strategy #4
## Buy Properties in Rebounding High Growth Markets

This strategy involves researching markets that exhibit high growth potential for value creation opportunities. Value investors uncover the next great place to be and buy properties in good locations. Many markets are primed to rebound from tough times and create great opportunities to get there before everyone else does. Be forward thinking and beat the crowd to expect growth opportunities.

Look for market inefficiencies where valuations have dropped much farther than market fundamentals support. Emotions and confidence play a huge part on property valuations so finding the imbalance can be a great value creation opportunity for value investors.

### *Case Study*

*Strategic Storage Trust is a private REIT that buys storage facilities around the country. They focus on buying high end storage properties in growing markets.*

**Subject:** *Augusta Ranch Storage*
*9252 E. Guadalupe Rd, Mesa, Arizona 85212*
**Property Description:** *Built in 2002, six single-story buildings on 4.62 acres, 570 Units, 75,600 Net Rentable Square Feet*
**Class & Occupancy**: *Class A Property, 81% Occupied*
**Purchase Price:** *$3,675, 000*
**Rehab Cost:** *None*
**Cap Rate/Financing/Lev. %:** *9.21% Cap rate, Loan Assumption, 5.38% Interest rate, 30 yr Amortization*

**Value strategy / Opportunity:** *Property was purchased at favorable pricing within a soft market with high future growth expected. No capital improvements were needed, but a management opportunity existed to create additional value.*

*VALUE INVESTOR PROFILE*
*An Interview with Michael Brennan*

# Position Your Company to Capitalize on the Distressed Industrial Real Estate Market

Michael Brennan uncovers time-tested strategies top executives and private investors must manage to properly position a real estate company to capitalize on today's distressed real estate market. Mr. Brennan has orchestrated more than $10 billion in industrial real estate transactions in the course of his 25 year career. Often sought as an industry expert on industrial real estate, Mr. Brennan has appeared on CNBC, CNNfn and Bloomberg Television.

**You've been quoted as saying, "This is the best buying opportunity in a generation." Where do you see the opportunities in this space?**

Well, I've been saying it's the best buying opportunity for a generation, but the last two years, we haven't seen that much for a lot of reasons. I think we will. When there's disruption in the capital markets, when there's disruption in the demand for space, and there is so much significant over-capacity, at some point, something's got to give.

There was a cease-fire called by the government, the FDIC and GAP, in which it changed how banks would recognize losses on existing portfolios. I think it's good the government did that because it would be anarchy if it didn't. Those properties are waiting for the right moment more banks can actually dispose of them where they have the earnings to do so.

On the CMBS side, those special servicers are waiting to hire the capacity to be able to deal with the REO's that they have. They also had some legal issues. So the stage is being set to be able to see a lot of properties come on the market that need a value-add opportunity. It was so big that we had to declare a cease-fire. It was so big that the FDIC decided not to handle it in the way they handled the Resolution Trust Corporation before. Now rather than taking over a bank, they sold banks pursuant to loss sharing agreements. But there's no question that I think that this space is going to be replete with opportunities. But it's also good, though.

I'm not an advocate that all of it should be coming on the market at one time. I don't think that it would be right. But I do think we'll be able to see some opportunities. How long does it last? I think it probably lasts as long as the buying opportunities existed back in the early '90s. From 1992 to 1996-7, it was easy to buy on a 10-cap rate. So if the hangover's proportional to the party, and there were 14 years of uninterrupted credit, you can expect the buying opportunities to last 5 or 6 years.

## How do you position your company to take advantage of this opportunity?

First of all, I think it takes a little perspective. It takes a belief. And if you don't have the belief, you're not exerting yourself every day, and you're not investing in the company's infrastructure. Having been in the business since 1979, I believe it's a cyclical business, and I believe this cycle will take its normal course. I think it sort of begins there. I have a belief that this is going to be the best buying opportunity because all the things that create buying opportunities are present here. It begins with that.

The second thing it begins with is to set high standards for what you want to do. If you're a value investor, presumably you're looking for good values, and therefore, good returns. You have to set your standards high because you're going to go through a lot of frustrating moments like we've gone through before, where you threw a party and nobody came. You don't find enough things to buy. So I think it's set the standards.

Third, set the expectations for the group that this is going to be a tough go. Even when we buy something now, we have to go and lease it. That's not going to be pretty. I've told the people that work for us it's not a waste of time to study a building, make an offer, and get turned down. Let's do that 100 times. When they are ready, we'll know a lot about the building, the sub-markets, and we'll be an expert in the market. So it's never really a waste of time unless you quit prematurely.

The last thing, I suppose, is to educate capital on why you're doing it, and why you're doing it that way. Believing that there's an opportunity, get down to the market and do it, rather than talk about it. Talk is not helpful to action. Tell investors what you're doing and show them what you've got, and then something good will happen.

### When you size up a deal, what are 3 or 4 things a good deal must have to fit in your portfolio?

I forget who it was that said this. I actually borrowed the line from him. He said, "There's only 3 or 4 things that matter in a deal, and the rest is noise." So you read these big books about how many barges are coming down the canal. It's all very meaningless.

There are four things that matter for us, and we actually have something called, "The Four Things that Matter." We look at where's it at. If it's a good in-fill industrial location, okay, so far, so good. The second thing we look for is functional qualities that are appropriate for the sub-market. A large bulk building in Tampa is not appropriate for the sub-market, but it might be very appropriate in the inland empire. Third thing is a discount to replacement cost. And, the fourth thing is income in place. Those are "The Four Things that Matter." So if we've got good income, we've got good function, we've got a good location, and we're buying below intrinsic value, the deal should work out.

### Do you prefer multi-tenant type buildings?

I do. All things being equal, there's always safety in numbers, and if it's multi-tenant, it generally tends to be smaller, which generally allows, for example, shoe leather to lease a building. If it's got a million square feet, we've got to wait until people want to buy a million square feet of Nike shoes. That's just a macroeconomic event. Whereas, leasing of smaller spaces, 20 to 50,000 square feet, is shoe leather, hustle, and you know, as well as the general economy.

The other thing is that we also prefer buildings that are built to service a major consumption zone, as opposed to supply it. The buildings in the Inland Empire are built because there are large consumption zones there. I'm talking about things that replenish Los Angeles or things that replenish Chicago, like a beverage company, or a vending company, or a food company, or somebody that's stocking up the stores as they're selling stuff on Michigan Avenue.

Those buildings really operate like apartment buildings, almost. Their desirability should grow as the demographics and the income grow. That's in stark contrast to these large, big boxes that are built based on a logistic plan, based upon a manufacturing plant in China, based upon a freight management plan or a rail management plan that can change, and that's going through changes right now. They're affected by changes in material handling equipment. They're affected by changes and improvements in point of sale technology.

All those forces are bearing down on those buildings' absorption and causing us to think that maybe these buildings are not suitable for our portfolio. I think those buildings are in harm's way as technology improves, whereas the buildings in close proximity, on the periphery of major consumption zones, that are smaller in size, operate in the same way apartments do, or small stores, or office buildings that serve sort of a downtown area.

**Michael, a critical component to building your company's platform was to team up with a capital partner.**

We know that one capital source may not accommodate all of the things that, as a value investor, we believe are appropriate to invest in.

I'll give you an example; institutions generally like acquisitions of $20 million, or say, $10 million and over. So on larger transactions, we've teamed up with institutions or funds that represent institutions.

Things between $10 million and $2 million, we recently sent out a press release on a capital source called Barnett Capital, which is a family office for one of the main shareholders of Medline Industries. The principals of Barnett are entrepreneurial and tremendously knowledgeable about value investing, and we told them that inasmuch as institutions don't want to buy from $2 to $10 million, but because there is a tremendous void in capital, it would be a wonderful opportunity. So we've hooked up, and we've done those deals.

The third source of capital is my own capital and the capital of the partners. Sometimes, the institutions will want to pass on something that we think is good. Sometimes Barnett Capital will pass on things that they don't think are appropriate for their strategy, but we might feel that a particular transaction is something that we, nevertheless, do believe in and want to pursue it. So those would generally be under $10 million.

The Gordian Knot that we're trying to cut is how do we find volume, and how do we find return as well? When you step up the volume, the return comes down. When you want to go after return, you have to go to smaller things. We're trying to build a large national industrial portfolio in five major markets, and the average building size in our industry is 100,000 square feet. So if it's at 40 bucks a foot, that's 4 million dollars a transaction.

We're setting up buckets of capital in recognition that there are different investment styles; there are different cut-off points for volume; and yet, the reason we have three is because we have a belief that if we aggregate these transactions and aggregate them in major markets, that someday we can roll those up like we did with First Industrial and create enormous value for the people that are our partners.

**Today, with the way the economy is right now, what critical organizational infrastructure should real estate companies be adopting to set themselves up for success tomorrow?**

They need a group of people that are dedicated to sourcing investment opportunities. They need a core group of people that are out there every day just doing that. When we used to open up an office at First Industrial, it took us probably a year to a year and a half to get on the board. That's because you have to begin to develop a pipeline. You have to tell your brokers, who you have a relationship with, what your criteria is. You have to develop credibility. You have to sort through a number of acquisitions. It takes a long time.

You need to start now so that you can plant the seeds. You can make the offers, get them rejected, and come back and re-plow that same ground again, and you'll probably find acceptances. Probably not unlike if you try to sell somebody something, they say no and then come back.

The second thing is you have to acquaint capital with the strategy. Having a capital officer is just as important as an acquisition officer. Acquisition people can bring new ideas to capital guys, and the capital guys can go out and find it. The capital guys can bring new ideas from capital to the acquisition guys, and they can try to source it. They have a wonderful interplay if they're together with one another.

Often they're separated, as though those worlds are mutually independent but they're co-dependent on each other. So it's very important that those two, yin and yang, come together and work with each other.

The last thing is for the leader of the company to make it very clear that investors' money is more important than our own money, and that we would rather lose money ourselves than ever lose anybody else's money. If we lose our reputation, then we really don't have anything.

**You co-founded First Industrial back in 1994, which went on to be a very large company. That was right at the bottom of the real estate cycle. Recently, you founded a new company**

**at a similar time in the real estate cycle. What lessons did you learn, and what successes did you have during the last cycle that you applied this time around?**

To get in the game and stay in the game. The other thing that I learned is the importance of having acquisition partners that have truly been industrial people most of their adult lives. People underestimate the historical knowledge and the historical relationships that are important in generating acquisitions, leasing, and sales. The best people at First Industrial, in terms of our acquisition personnel, were people that had those characteristics.

If they were analytically gifted and skilled, while that was important, it would take them many years before they developed relationships that would actually turn into consummated transactions, and then consummated sales. We learned we were taking a big risk if we hired somebody who had the intellectual capacity but not the on-the-ground experience in the field. And I didn't appreciate that until we went through over 50 regional directors in the 35 offices that we had over the course of 15 years. The number one thing that they didn't have was deep relationships and a deep involvement in the sector or in the field for a long time.

There was one other common denominator. If they were so good, they could go off and get the capital themselves. But that was a small group, but I'd say 90% of the common denominator was no acclimation to the market. You have to like associating with people like that. We want people that want to hang out with the industrial personnel in their field and they enjoy that and find that to be stimulating and interesting.

**What big mistakes do you see investors making when trying to buy in today's market?**

Lack of patience and/or allowing an investment to be consummated on low probability assumptions are big mistakes. In the heyday, people said, "Well, I'm going to bid $100 million, and I'm going to assume rents go up at 6%, occupancy's at 96% –

going to stay at 96%, tenants are going to renew at a rate of 75%, and cap rates are going to stay at about 6%."

Well, what are the odds that all four of those things happen? If you go back to probability in school, the first odds that you're going to have rents going to grow at 6% - it only happened twice in 30 years. So I'd say it's at least a 14 out of 15 chance that it's 'not' going to happen.

Now multiply that by the next assumption you made, and you've got the worst deal you've ever seen in your lifetime. When you sign off on low probability assumptions, that's what gets deals in trouble. It's the assumption page that's more important than anything else.

When we look at deals, we say, "What are the odds that you're going to actually retain 70%?" Aren't the odds almost 95% that you'll never do that? Isn't it more like 60%? So I think that's one of the things you have to do. The acquisition guys will say, "Yeah, if you do that, you'll never buy anything." And we say, "Well, then, take it out on the seller. Be a good salesman and go and take it out on the seller. You tell him that it's his cross to bear, not ours, because you're a steward for somebody else's money."

**Michael Brennan**
Co-Founder, Brennan Investment Group

Michael Brennan is Co-Founder and Chairman of Brennan Investment Group, headquartered in Chicago, Illinois. Brennan Investment Group is a private value real estate investment firm that acquires, develops and operates industrial properties in select major metropolitan markets throughout the United States.

Prior to forming Brennan Investment Group, Mr. Brennan co-founded First Industrial Realty Trust in 1994 where he helped build the company to over 85 million square feet before he left in 2008. Mr. Brennan has orchestrated more than $10 billion in industrial real estate transactions in the course of his 25 year career.

# Chapter 6

## *Advanced Strategies for Real Estate Value Investors*

*"We bought a 100-unit complex in Benton, Texas, and rebranded it as Vintage Pads, and went after the student market at the University of North Texas, in a very defined and targeted way. And through that, what we found was it was a C asset, but it was in a great location with great frontage. It was two and a half blocks from the university, and we were able to basically change their exterior appearance, redo all 100 interior units with our green upgrade program, and we were able to take NOI from about $425,000 to just over $1 million annualized over the last 19 months."*

Bill Bennett
Iconic Development

Creating value can be a very complex process that involves an expert team of professionals to get a value investor through the process. The advanced strategies in this chapter require a deep and narrow specialization in each strategy. One mishap or wrong decision can cause serious time setbacks and cost a lot of money. The upside to specializing in one of the advance strategies is there is limited competition from other real estate professionals. When assessing whether to engage in one of these strategies, make sure you properly consider the expertise and knowledge required to successfully execute the strategy. While the profit potential may be enticing, the downside could be bigger.

For investors that are stepping up from strategies outlined in the previous chapter, start small and grow into bigger deals.

Because the competition is limited, there are numerous opportunities once you build a platform.

Some of these strategies are better used early in the real estate cycle's recovery process and others better used later in the cycle. Being earlier to the party rather than later will better increase your chances of success.

## Strategy #5
## Convert Properties to Other Higher and Better Uses

Many old industrial buildings, warehouses, office buildings, churches, service stations, car lots, and housing units are ripe for recycling into other innovative and better uses. Repurposing buildings offers value investors the opportunity to create value from underutilized assets. With the high vacancy around the country in various submarkets, there is ample opportunity to convert unused structures into new and in-demand opportunities.

The condo conversion craze is well documented, but did you ever drive by and see a boarded up old motel, a corner gas station fenced, an empty bank on the corner, or an empty car lot? Sure you have. These are future opportunities waiting to be discovered and converted into higher and better use assets.

The real key to having success converting these types of buildings is to uncover potential users in the area that are in demand for a specific use. Finding the future buyer or tenant begins the process. With the user in mind, better yet in hand, engage a real estate consulting firm to conduct a feasibility study to find out if there is demand. If there is a demand, you will then need to engage an architect and engineer to plan the process and make sure the land use and the building codes allow such a conversion. If the new conversion solves a problem for the area and others connected to the property, then most likely you'll find success. Make sure you are solving a problem.

### Converting an Old Office Building

An old office building void of tenants was located next to a thriving hospital. The building's elevator system was antiquated, the roof was in bad shape and the HVAC system was inoperable. A value investor friend of mine with ingenuity bought the building for land cost and converted it into medical offices for local doctors that needed to be close to the hospital. It took 2 years for the building to be converted and leased but with a high occupancy. The investment paid off handsomely for the investor.

### Converting Large Single Use Retail Use to Multi-Tenant Use

I interviewed a gentleman named Skyler Hynes recently who was hired by the property owner of a 100,000 square foot Mervyn's retail center suffering from extremely high vacancy. Skyler decided to convert his building to multi-tenant use. The interior of the building was converted into a small retail mall for local business owners who needed a place to sell their retail items. The entire vacant space was divided into several 600 square foot spaces. The cost of renovation was about $1 million or the same cost it would have been to give a single user in tenant improvements. In the end for this investment, the sum of the parts exceeded the whole by generating much more income with multi-tenants than with one big user.

## Strategy #6
## Buy Distressed Troubled Loans and Notes

Large real estate funds have been created to buy portfolios of troubled loans. Many value investors find it easier to get control of a property through the debt side by buying a troubled loan in hopes of taking back the property through foreclosure. The term flying around the industry is "loan to own." This value strategy is an opportunity for investors to purchase commercial loans individually or as a part of a larger portfolio at a significant discount to the face value of the note.

Another related strategy is to agree with the property owner to buy the property by getting the lender to agree to a loan reduction or short sale. This is very common in today's marketplace where new buyers are agreeing to purchase property that has a troubled loan and getting the lender to agree to a short sale.

Gary Sabin with Excel Trust recently purchased the note on a class A, 375,000 square foot shopping center in Birmingham, Alabama, at a big discount to the bank note of about $33.5 million. Gary told me, "It was in a very messy situation, so we bought the note, and because we had a relationship with the developer, we were able to work out a situation where we could kind of put Humpty Dumpty back together again, as opposed to the developer filing bankruptcy and just having a fight forever. Because we had a relationship with them, we were able to go with them, give them a participation, and purchase the property on a 10.3% cap rate. That did not include about 85,000 feet of vacant space that we didn't pay anything for."

When buying troubled loans, value investors need to surround themselves with experts in due diligence, real estate law, property management and third party consultation. As lenders sell their "trouble" to buyers, value investors need to be careful to inspect and investigate the trouble they are buying. Here's is potential list of problems to uncover:

- Property physical condition issues
- Promises in leases
- Title issues including liens
- Entity issues including authority
- Loan document issues including guaranty's
- Legal issues including pending lawsuits

Conducting a thorough due diligence and review on the physical, financial, and legal issues affecting the asset and loan will reduce future costly problems.

## Case Study

*The Magellan Group purchased a troubled note at a discount to the existing note creating significant value for the investor.*

**Subject:** *Grace Place Industrial Loan by Mesa West Real Estate Income Fund II, LP*
*City of Commerce, Los Angeles, CA*
**Property Description:** *1962, centrally located industrial building, 500,795 sq ft multi-tenant/ 30,350 sq ft single-tenant*
**Class & Occupancy:** *A Class Property, 100% leased (NNN) to 4 tenants*
**Purchase Price:** *The Magellan Group purchased the $45M ($84.73 psf) note for $32.2M ($60.62 psf). Mesa West Capital provided a $25.6M ($48.20 psf) senior mortgage loan for this property.*
**Rehab Cost:** *None*
**Cap Rate/Financing/Lev. %:**
*$25,600,000 Senior Loan*
*$  5,750,000 Mezzanine Loan*
*$     850,000 Investor Cash*

**Value Strategy / Opportunity:** *Value Real Estate Investor, The Magellan Group, purchased the $45M note for $32.2M, a 28.4% discount on a 100% leased, 531,000 sq ft industrial building. The as-is appraisal was $49,500,000, creating a significant value creation for The Magellan Group and a very safe loan for Mesa West Capital.*

## Strategy #7
## Buy and Add Additional Square Footage to Existing Property

Adding more square footage to a property is a value creation strategy many value investors use, especially developers. For simplicity purposes, let's say an investor owns a 3 bedroom, 2 bath single family rental home. The investor decides to add on an additional bedroom, creating a 4 bedroom, 2 bath house. By doing so, the investor has added more square footage to the home allowing for more livable space. The house will rent for more, and the resale value will be higher. In the end, the investor created value by adding on more square footage.

With land prices falling so much recently, shrewd value investors can find properties to buy with the potential to build additional square footage. Gary Sabin with Excel Trust has found that today many sellers are throwing in parcels of land for free along with the purchase of their retail properties.

Intrinsic value takes into account future cash flow and with the potential to increase cash flow through "making the pie bigger," value investors should be researching the potential of this strategy. These types of deals become hard to pencil as property valuation get stronger.

When looking for new acquisitions, consider the option of adding more square footage. Think outside the box and be creative. Here is a list to get you thinking about ways to generate more income:

- Build storage units
- Build garages
- Build upward on existing structures
- Extend buildings outward
- Purchase adjoining land to build
- Demolish part or all of an old building and build a new structure

## Case Study

*Gary Sabin of Excel Realty Trust purchased a class A retail power center with strategy of adding more square footage. With the low purchase price and adding more square footage, Gary created significant value.*

**Subject:** *Plaza at Rockwood, Rockwood, Texas*
*Rockwall, a suburb of Dallas, is the 2nd wealthiest county in Texas and was the 3rd fastest growing county in the nation over the past decade according to the U.S. Census Bureau.*

**Property Description:** *332,000 square foot power center with tenants J.C. Penney, Dick Sporting Goods, Staples, Best Buy and*

*Belk Department Store; 80,000 square foot; phase II under construction with 60% leased.*
**Class & Occupancy**: *A Class Property, Phase I 100% leased*
**Purchase Price:** *$41 million including land to build out phase II*
**Rehab Cost:** *None*
**Cap Rate/Financing/Lev. %:** *Cash*

**Value Strategy / Opportunity:** *Purchase off market power center with additional land to build 80,000 more square feet. Purchased class A property at class B pricing with the potential of adding substantial value.*

## Strategy #8
## Buy Property and Reposition to Target Niche Tenant Base

This is one of my favorite strategies, and one that I've used a lot. As Steven Covey, author of *7 Habits of Highly Effective People*, said, "Start with the end in mind." Find a hungry crowd and serve their needs. Think about this. Most developers build properties and then try to figure out who they are going to market the space to. Also, don't most inventors of products create products, and then try and sell them?

This all sounds backwards to me. Here's my idea: Conduct research and understand the problems of a niche group and then offer a solution to that niche group in the way of a product. By scratching the itch, marketing the product or space becomes easier and creates lots of value where there is much more pricing power.

Value investors using this strategy must be good at researching and uncovering problems in the marketplace. By conducting solid research, you can find gaps in the market and underserved needs of a niche group. Once you find a problem within a niche group, you reposition the property with a lifestyle to solve the niche tenant base's problems. The solution will include targeted property features, amenities and services. Once you tailor your property, you essentially have no competition in the marketplace. With no "direct" competition, you will have much higher rents and strong resident retention. Most of my properties generate 25% higher rents because of the lifestyle I have created on my properties. Add all that up and this strategy is a real value creation machine.

I got a call from Bill Bennett of Iconic Development, telling me he had heard about me through a real estate broker in San Antonio, Texas. I was in San Antonio back in mid-2008 trying to buy a 399-unit apartment building. I specialize in creating Hispanic themed properties that solve living problems for my target customer base. This particular property, called Spanish Trace, was located in a great location but it needed a lot of work. After doing extensive rent comparable surveys in the immediate trade area, I determined rents at Spanish Trace could be raised $100 to $150 per unit based on unit type, after I completed my $5 million niche targeted renovation. I had an equity joint venture partner lined up, had the debt financing lined up and was ready to close. Two weeks before the closing, the financial markets crashed in mid-September, 2008. My lender raised our interest rate 150 basis points (1.5%) essentially killing the deal.

Now I'm on the phone will Bill in mid-2010, whom I hadn't even known, and he tells me, "I bought Spanish Trace." Bill had heard about my plans for the property and decided to investigate the property. Since his company had previous experience using the same niche strategy, he saw the opportunity and bought the property. Bill added most of the features, amenities and services I planned on. He's getting higher rents and the property is well occupied. After I got off the phone with him, I was very happy to learn that a nice person like Bill saw the vision I had and turned Spanish Trace into a jewel.

Like myself, my now good friend Bill, uses this strategy very effectively. His has a few niche groups he specializes in: students, Hispanics, Echo-boomers and seniors. Visit his website to get a flavor of the types of amazing things he's doing in the marketplace at www.IconicDevelopment.com.

## Case Study

*Bill Bennett of Iconic Development purchased an apartment building and repositioned the property to a Hispanic themed property.*

**Subject:** *Spanish Trace Apartments (renamed property: Rayo del Sol Apartments)*
*7226 Blanco Road, San Antonio, TX*
**Property Description:** *399 units, 15 acres, 303,000 rentable square feet; 40 years of age – primarily serving workforce housing type tenants (non-subsidized)*
**Class & Occupancy**: *"C" asset in "A" location, currently 90% occupied*
**Purchase Price:** *$10.85 million, closed 12/18/2009*
**Rehab Cost:** *$3 million, over 32 month period*
**Cap Rate/Financing/Lev. %:** *9% cap rate on in place operations at acquisition, 5.71% financing at 50% project leverage*

**Value Strategy / Opportunity:** *Added amenities (playground, clubhouse, business center, after school program, soccer field, BBQ pavilion) to cater to Hispanic families and update the interior of all 399 units. Increased average rent from $.68/sf to $.79/sf in a $.82/sf rent comparable submarket. Plan to sell a portion of the land to adjacent Lexus dealership to generate additional income, and to lower operating expenses through Iconic's green upgrade program. Project goal is to deliver approximate 11% yield on unlevered cost, 20%+ IRR, and 2x+ cash multiple over four year investment horizon.*

# *Repositioning Properties to a Niche Tenant Base*

Iconic Development is a real estate investment firm that specializes in buying 'C' multifamily properties in 'A' locations within strategically identified submarkets, and then they reposition their properties to a niche tenant base such as students, echo boomers, seniors and the Hispanic market. This strategy has allowed Bill to consistently generate high returns for his investors where average rents are 25% higher than his competition, even in today's tough market.

**You're a true value investor on many fronts. Tell us about your overall investment strategy and how it's different.**

Our investment strategy is to invest in demographically-driven niche apartments. What that means for us, is customer bases that are unique and underserved, like students, seniors, and Hispanic families. By going after a precisely targeted group, you can better understand your customer base, what they want, and better cater the real estate product and the operating program directly to them.

We feel like in those niche apartment areas, other people are scared of it. But if you're really learning your customer base, you can provide a better, differentiated product that out-competes your competition. While we are competing for a smaller slice of the pie, our lease-signing rates are typically two to three "X" where our competitive properties. A normal apartment-seeker goes out and looks at five apartments in their search, and kind of by definition, about 20% of the time, they're choosing our apartment. We usually lease 40 to 60% out of our overall prospects.

**You're buying multifamily properties and repositioning them towards a certain niche. You then create an environment around the property, and then market that in the marketplace, and your message is met with those types of renters that fit the demographics that you're going after.**

Yes, that's exactly right. We're just the highly-targeted apartment offering similar to what the hotel industry evolved to in the late '90s and early 2000s, which was when the boutique hotel concept took off, and the people that did it well, they really found it to be a great niche. We're seeing, by applying those same types of concepts to apartments – i.e., high design, better amenities, a better service and operating program that it blows the doors off of the beige carpet, white wall apartment, which is like eating rice out of a takeout box with a glass of lukewarm water. We think our apartments are more like jasmine rice with green curry prawns, a mojito, and a side of sri raja.

**What other tenant niches do you work on other than Hispanics?**

Students are our largest demographic that we serve. We're the largest landlord around Boise State University. We're at the University of North Texas and Texas State. We spend a lot of time doing research into the demographic, and we have models that rank the different markets for attractiveness. What drew us to those markets outside of Chicago was they have growing gaps between supply and demand. Specifically, most of them have an under-represented, kind of professional ownership in the class C apartment space. What we're really doing in that market is we're finding C product in an A location, and we're rehabbing it to earn B rents.

The students housing business is firing on all cylinders. As the economy's been tough, it seems like kids are staying in school longer. The demographics of it are already super-strong, if you're in the right states, metros, and markets. That business has been just a tremendous growth opportunity for us, and our investors in those projects are calling us, asking if there is more.

For student apartments, we've got eight apartments in the state of Texas, and then we've got three apartments in and around Boise State in the state of Idaho. And so we're primarily focused on those states and metro areas and universities that have very high growth and not much in the way of new construction.

## Can you give us an example of a property you repositioned?

We bought a 100-unit complex in Denton, Texas, and rebranded it as Vintage Pads, and went after the student market at the University of North Texas, in a very defined and targeted way. And through that, what we found was it was a C asset, but it was in a great location with great frontage.

It was two and a half blocks from the university, and we were able to basically change their exterior appearance, redo all 100 interior units with our green upgrade program, and we were able to take NOI from about $425,000 to just over $1 million annualized over the last 19 months.

It's a pretty terrible time right now in the real estate business, and it just goes to show you that, if you're really focused, and you find the right assets that you can do something with and focus heavily on executing, you can create value through any market cycle.

## The real difference is you're buying something at a good price, in the right location, for the right demographics, and you're just catering towards them.

We think about value investing as basically, you're trying to buy wholesale, and you're capturing value at the beginning, during the purchase price. And then, you're able to do something with it to create value. Then you're going to capture it again in the form of a refinancing or a sale while paying great cash dividends.

The Denton, Texas, project is in the high teen's cash on cash returns in under two years, which is better than we thought we'd do. Part of the really great thing about catering to niches is that you can push the envelope. We were able to do some pretty neat things with this asset to help increase value, like converting storage units into actual leasable units.

We saw that there was basically no product in the market for the very high end, so we created several penthouse units. We were able to boost rents to $1,000 per month, and they were the first units to lease. And so, there are always gaps in the marketplace, and if you can identify those gaps, you have the chance of certain profitability.

### What are some big challenges you've had repositioning niche tenant base assets?

The biggest challenge we usually face is the type of renter who rents a product at $500 is different from the one that rents it at $625. And so, within our student housing business, we see about 80% of the tenants turn over during the reposition. Even though you're providing a superior offering and better quality, it's just a different renter profile.

So that puts intense pressure on the leasing and marketing to sign many new leases – your presence where they're moving up because they choose to, or in some cases, if your renewals are strong in the second year, you're forcing evictions so you can complete your business plan.

### What matrix do you use to identify favorable markets for your investments?

Market selection is one of the biggest things we think about. As a company that's looking to out-perform, the market selection is at the heart of the issue. What we're looking for are markets that have strong demographics first of all, and then, particularly within the student housing space, they have growing demand without the same growth in supply, and where we see a an underserved niche, and the kind of product we can get out it. We primarily focus on repositioning C assets in A locations, and so some of the newer markets don't have that, but most of the university markets out there do.

**Give us a flavor of what it looks like in a unit that you've redone – some of the colors, maybe some of the amenities, and so forth.**

One of the things we see when we're buying assets, primarily from mom & pops, is that they don't have great design, they don't have a website, and they often don't have any kind of online marketing strategy, and that's a major portion of how the students pick their properties.

An example of what you see, like in the Denton, Texas, project, you walk in and the first thing you see is artisan-stained concrete flooring. Replacing carpet is an environmentally-friendly thing. Not only that, but you don't have to replace the carpet all the time in the unit turns, it looks better, and gets higher rent than the competing properties. It's just really great from an owner's perspective because the units don't get that bad carpet smell, and you can turn them faster, so you're creating cash flow, both on the revenue and expense side.

Then you'll see a vibrant color wall. We tend to focus on making a splash when folks first move in with some great countertops or some designer backsplash tile. We usually end up putting in some beautiful lighting system and just focus on modernizing the apartment and making it feel and look like the generation we're targeting wants.

**What types of attributes – like features, size, location, price, etc. – does a property need to have so it fits within your investment strategy?**

We love the $5 to $15 million dollar apartment space. It's too big for the mom & pops; it requires too much money and too much skill. It's too small for the private equity funds and the REIT's, and too much work for them, frankly.

We get paid to do that heavy lifting. We target C assets in A locations in A markets that can be repositioned up a notch.

And what that typically means is we're able to raise rents 20 to 25%, on average, across the units, through our rebranding, repositioning, unit interior rehab, and we've been successful doing that in over 800 units now. And it's gone really great.

## Do you prefer properties that have higher vacancy so it's easier to get in and turn units?

We're actually the opposite. We're trying to buy assets that are 90% to 100% full, and even if you did nothing, it would be a great investment. That limits our investors and our downside risk. Another thing about buying an asset that's full or nearly full is you know that the rents are below market if it's in a great location.

We tend to purchase the '70s and '80s built product. They usually have larger floor plans and you've got a better palette to work with. They're usually in better locations, so you're not really taking the market risk and you're not on the fringe of society. You're close to the demand drivers. You're betting on a proven market. But typically, there's severe deferred maintenance and a lot of TLC and hard work that it takes to bring it up a notch.

## So you're putting money into the properties per your business plan. How much do you spend per unit?

It ranges from $10,000 to $15,000 on average, depending on the property age and condition. We've had some units that we've put $35,000 to $40,000 into, where we've added bedrooms and bathrooms. We've built some new units, converted some units out of storage sheds, combined units, and taken units apart. A lot of the benefit of dealing with a '70s/'80s vintage product is you have very large units, so there's greater number of things that you can do with them.

Overall, what you're really trying to do is focus on the fundamental competitive landscape and the market, and trying to see how you can differentiate your product. So some of your product may cater to 19 and 20-year-old girls; some of it may cater to upperclassmen males, and you're just trying to match the amenity, the operating program, and the real estate look, to the target audience, within the demographic, which is very focused. We try to take it down a notch and really understand who's living there and why.

**You're buying property that typically has low rents; you're upgrading the property with improvements; and you're niching it towards a certain tenant base. What types of rent increases do you get on a percentage basis, compared to your competition?**

The competition shifts throughout the life cycle. There's one competitive landscape, which is typically the other mom & pop apartments with no amenities and kind of bare bones look and feel at a pretty low rent level.

What we usually end up competing with is the much newer product that has great amenities, but is in typically a much worse location and has smaller units. We end up trying to have the value proposition of, we've got units that are bigger, closer, and cheaper but they're still pretty cool. They're maybe 20% below the top of the market rents, so they can't come down and compete with us. And we just gradually have been stealing their tenants and doing a great job in this economy.

**So you're 20% below the top A properties, the newer properties. The lower end C properties, how much are you above them?**

20% to 25%. Particularly in Texas, there wasn't a lot of product built between the mid-'80s and 2000 due to the oil bust, and so there's not a lot of B product out there in the market. So we're taking C product and really pouring money into it to create that gap that's out there in the marketplace.

**Bill Bennett**
Co-Founder, Iconic Development

Bill spent six years as an engineer, project manager and as a direct manager at Active Power, a green energy company that went from a zero revenue start-up to a publicly traded company. Bill has been a successful principal real estate investor over the past eight years, has worked for two real estate private equity funds, was one of three members of a senior housing developer with over $400 million of product under development, and owns a profitable student housing brokerage. Bill is a member of the Urban Land Institute and Pension Real Estate Association, and is a faculty member in the Kellogg School of Management's Real Estate Program.

# PART
# 2

# Chapter 7

## Unleashing the Value Hound:
## Playing the Game of
## Real Estate Value Investing

*"So one way or another, we keep loading ourselves to see value, and when you can see value – when you innately, inside yourself, know – then that's really the key to any deal."*

Steven Fogel
Westwood Financial

Let's take a journey together. I am going to take you through the entire process, from beginning to end, on how to play the game of real estate value investing. We are going to see the good, bad and the ugly. We are going to see the reality of this game. It's not a get rich quick game. Rance King of RK Properties, who has built his real estate investment business to over $300 million during the last thirty plus years, calls the real estate value investing game, "A get rich slowly game." If you look at this game as a long term process where you are always taking steps forward, slow consistent steps forward by keeping it simple, you will attain significant wealth for your retirement. Unlike the stock market, you are in control of the game, every step of the way. So, sit back and let's take the journey together.

## Creating Your Investment Business Plan

The very first thing you need to decide on is your goals. What do you want to achieve from your real estate investments? How long do you want to play the game? Where do you want to play the game? Before you undertake this process, you need to put together a road map of the trip you want to take. Where does the trip start and end? What things do you want to see along the trip? Too many investors jump into the game without knowing what it is they are doing, and why.

Take Steven Covey's advice, "Start with the end in mind." Decide on the end game and work backwards. It's amazing how often I use this advice. For example, when I decided to write this book, I started with the end in mind. I sat down on my chair with a blank yellow pad and asked myself, "What do I want readers to take away from this book?" After thinking and twisting things around for awhile, I wrote down two things I wanted readers to take away from this book. First, I wanted to expose what real estate value investing was all about. Second, I wanted to show the process involved with real estate value investing and how someone can use that process to create long term wealth. In the end, I wanted readers to understand the real estate value investing game and have a process to play the game.

After having the end in mind, next I created an outline of the steps I needed to take to reach my end point. The steps I created were the chapters. This book has a starting point, beginning with the first chapter, and it has an ending point with the last chapter. You can do the same thing with your real estate investment business plan by sitting down and deciding on where you want to end up and then plotting your trip from a beginning point, following a path to that end point.

## 11 Reasons to Prepare an Investment Business Plan

There are many reasons as to why a business plan should be prepared. Regardless of the specific reason, the underlying goal of preparing a business plan is to insure the success of the business. A business plan:

1. Provides you with the road map that you need in order to run your business and plan your apartment investment. It

allows you to make detours, change directions, and alter the pace that you set in starting or running the business.

2. Assists in financing. Investor and lenders want to see that you know where you are, where you are going, and how you are going to get there.
3. Tells you how much money you need, when you will need it, and how you are going to get it.
4. Helps you to clearly think through the competitive advantage of your rental business that you are buying, and allows you to consider every aspect of that business.
5. Raises the questions that you need to have answered in order to succeed in your business.
6. Establishes a system of checks and balances for your business so that you avoid mistakes.
7. Sets up benchmarks to keep your business under control.
8. Helps you develop the competitive spirit to make you keenly prepared and ready to operate.
9. Makes you think through the entire business process so that you do not begin a new acquisition blindly, or lack vital information in buying and operating your property.
10. Forces you to analyze the market and business climate.
11. Gives you a "go" or "no go" answer about buying a property.

**Getting Started**

Since there are 31 flavors of ice cream and everyone likes different flavors, the choice comes down to your personal desire. Do you want to be actively involved with the day to day business of real estate investing, or do you want your real estate investment business to be secondary to your profession and career? Maybe you want some combination of the two. If you are a more experienced real estate investor, then building a real estate business makes sense in a full time capacity, assuming you are well capitalized. If you are a new investor, then starting your real estate business as a part-time endeavor, a more passive activity, is right for you. This is a long journey that requires experience to be successful so I recommend starting your journey part-time until you gain the expertise, knowledge and experience.

Later in Chapter 10, we will be taking a look at Rance King, who built his real estate business from the ground up. He started his real estate investment business passively while working as a business machine salesman in Long Beach. While he was working, he bought his first property, a four-plex. As he gained experience and felt comfortable, he quit his job and started RK Properties in 1976. Getting started in the real estate business can take many forms, but Rance's approach is a great model for many investors; it's up to you.

## Pick Your Specialization

To be good at something, you need to specialize. To truly see and recognize value, you need to be an expert. As a value real estate investor, you will need to specialize in a property type, a market and a value creation strategy to be successful. Warren Buffet is regularly approached with investment opportunities and he quickly declines them, in part, because he doesn't understand the business. He specializes in certain business types and sticks with them. You too must specialize and become an expert in something.

**Property type:** There is any number of property types to pick from, such as houses, apartment buildings, retail centers, office buildings, industrial building, storage units, warehouse buildings and hotels. Find a property type that compliments your personality.

**Market:** Pick a part of town where you see opportunities to execute your value creation strategy. Don't go too far from home base. As an expert, you will know everything about this market from whose coming and going to the people that make things happen in your market.

**Value creation strategy**: Learn and become an expert at executing one of the value creation strategies outlined in this book. To begin, pick a simple strategy. As you gain experience, you will be able to combine multiple strategies.

## Creating Your Acquisition Criteria

Through the development of your specialization, you will be able to create your acquisition criteria. Your acquisition criteria must be clear and concise. It spells out exactly the type of property investment you are looking for. Visit websites of leading value investors mentioned in this book and you will see a page with their acquisition criteria describing the types of investment properties they are actively seeking. Here's a short list of items to include in your acquisition criteria sheet:

- Property type
- Property size range (dollar, square footage, or # of units)
- Property characteristics (condition, features, class.)
- Desired markets
- Financing (Assumable, new, etc.)
- Special situations (low rents, deferred maintenance, high vacancy)

Why do you need to create an acquisition criteria sheet? The acquisition sheet will be your calling card. Send this sheet to real estate brokers or anyone else that needs to understand the type of investment deals you're doing. Ideally, you will send this sheet out to a multitude of people trying to find deals.

## Building Your Team of Experts

Surround yourself with great people. To find the best deals, finance and close deals, you need a team of experts that you can lean on to help in your business. When it comes to adding people on your team, be unemotional and get the best players. You may have a brother or friend that's in the business, but if they're not the very best, don't put them on your team. I can't stress enough to seek out the best players to put on your team because value creation requires expertise. Barry Nalebuff said it best, "Creating value is inherently cooperative, capturing value is inherently competitive."

There are many business and real estate experts you will want on your team but here are the most important experts you will need:

- Real estate attorney
- Real estate broker
- Loan broker
- Equity raiser
- Property manager
- Support network

The very essence of value real estate investing is finding great deals and getting them financed so that you can close on them. During that process, you need professionals that will help you find, finance and close deals. Except for a property manager, most of your team is dedicated to helping execute the acquisition. Once you close on a deal, you need "the best" property manager in town to execute your value creation plan. Search high and low until you uncover the best property management company because 70% of management companies suck.

Build a support network of professionals that you can go to for advice. Steven Fogel in his book, *The Yes I Can Guide to Mastering Real Estate*, recommends investors build a free board of directors that gives you counsel and advice. Many real estate brokers, managers and other investors are happy to offer advice to you, free of charge. Use your support network as a sounding board on tough decision. You will be surprised at the quality of help you will get from some of the smartest minds in the business, if you just ask.

## Uncovering Value Investment Opportunities

It's time to jump into your value hound suit. You are a full-fledged value hound on a relentless mission to look in every nook and cranny to uncover value creation opportunities. You will sniff high and low looking for value. Do you feel it? I do and it's a part of who I am. You are in the club. A value hound!

My goal is to set your mind frame as a true value investor, just like the people you have read about in this book. That's who you are, a value investor that avoids the herd mentality, pays $.50 for a $1.00, understands that simple is better than complex, and acts on facts, not hunches. You are a value hound on a mission to find great value opportunities for you and your investors.

## Start Small

As a budding value hound, you need to start small. Value hounds need to learn how to walk before they run. Their noses, for sniffing out great deals, take time to develop. Learning a new environment, making new contacts and obtaining the skills it takes  to complete deals takes time. Since this is a long term process, there's no need to rush your business.

I was watching an episode of "*Blue Bloods*" with Tom Selleck one Friday night and he said something that caught my attention.  On this TV show, Tom is the police commissioner of the New York Police Department, and he was giving advice to a new cop who just left the police academy. This cop was getting frustrated because he was working alongside a senior police officer and they hadn't been involved in any big crime cases.  They were strictly working on the street, writing tickets and solving domestic disputes cases. Tom said to the cop, "You just left the police academy where you learned the skills to become a police officer. On the street, you get to use the new skills you learned at the academy. You will be working with another officer on small cases until you gain the experience." Isn't it really the same for a new value hound?

I know you want to do big deals.  They will come, but it's more important to the foundation of your career to perfect your investing skills and gain the experience of working on deals.

Working on smaller deals, early in your career, has its advantages because a smaller deal is easier to get done, quicker and cheaper to correct mistakes, easier to raise equity funds, builds skills and experience, easier to make contacts, builds confidence, and sets the stage for larger deals. When you go to an investor having never done a deal, it's hard to get them to give you money. However, if you have done a deal, even though it's a small deal, then you are much better positioned as the expert.

## Finding the Deal: Where to Look for Value Opportunities

You might have to look at 100 deals and negotiate on 10 deals to buy one, but you can find good deals, especially in this great buyer's market. Spending time looking at a lot of deals is necessary because not every deal that comes across your desk is a good deal. Even if the deal meets your investment criteria and you begin negotiating, there is no guarantee that you will end up with the property. The seller may be negotiating with another buyer and take their offer, or you may not want the deal after further research.

Here are some places to look for the "perfect" deal that meets your acquisition criteria:

**1. Real Estate Brokers**: Since real estate brokers are in the business of selling property and are a major source of deal flow, you should start building relationships with many brokers and agents in the area you want to invest. Make sure the brokers you work with specialize in the types of properties that are on your investment criteria list. Be persistent in following up and staying in touch with these brokers. The really good deals come from off market deals that are not listed, so you want to be on the list of buyers they call first.

**2. Loopnet.com:** This website is a property listing source of properties that are for sale nationwide. You can drill down on the type of property that fits your investment criteria. This is another good way to meet real estate brokers as they typically have the listing on Loopnet.com.

**3. Drive the Marketplace:** A couple times a week for an hour or two, you should drive the submarket you are interested in and search for properties that meet your investment criteria. Write down the name and address of the property. Contact a title company or local county records to obtain the contact information of the property owner. Send them a letter inquiring on their potential interest in selling their property. This is a great way of finding good deals that are off market.

**4. Local Newspapers/Websites:** Many property owners advertise their properties for sale in the local newspaper. Regularly, review the real estate section of the local newspaper to find potential properties for sale. I've found many deals this way and they turned out to be big winners.

**5. Send Letters to Property Owners:** Get a list of property owners in your area that meet your target market and send them a letter inquiring on their potential interest in selling their property. Make sure to include your contact information so that they can call you.

**6. Send Flyers:** Send a flyer that lists your investment criteria to all real estate brokers and agents in your marketplace. Send this flyer at least once a month to stay in front of this source.

**7. Contact Property Management Companies:** Since management is their game, property management companies are a good source of leads on who is looking to sell their property. They can be incentivized by getting a real estate commission (seller would pay) and keeping management of the property upon sale.

**8. Get Leads From Real Estate Investment Clubs:** Many real estate investment clubs offer an exchange for its members who want to buy or sell property. There are many investors tired of being a landlord and need to sell their property. Attend one or more real estate investment clubs searching for leads to buy a property.

**9. Lending Institutions:** Many lending institutions have foreclosed properties (REO) that are for sale. Typically, these properties are listed with local real estate brokers. Contact your local banks and ask for their REO department. This is a good way to find the top agent dealing with most of the REO's.

**10. Subscribe to Foreclosure Service:** There are foreclosure services that list properties in foreclosure. You pay for this service to get a list of properties in foreclosure. Contact the property owners on this list and inquire on their interest of selling.

**11. Contact Local Vendors:** There are many vendors that service properties, such as carpet cleaners, landscapers, painters, plumbers, and many more. These vendors know which properties are paying their invoices late. Find out these properties and contact the property owners. They may be having trouble and may want to sell.

**12. Search the County Records for Code Violations:** There are many properties that are violating planning and environmental codes and are being poorly operated. Find out the properties and contact the property owners.

**13. Place Property Want Ads:** Create an ad that briefly describes your investment criteria and contact information and place an ad in the local newspaper or on the internet.

**14. Use Bird Dogs:** A bird dog is someone who comes into frequent contact with problem properties. Tenants, neighbors, mail carrier, trash collectors, delivery truck drivers, repairmen, and such are good bird dog candidates. Tell these types of people you are looking for problem properties and that you will pay them a finder's fee for information (i.e. $500).

Even though you have established a solid network of resources, there is no guarantee that deals will come quickly and easily. Do not get frustrated. It takes time for the seeds you planted to produce fruit. Make sure you continue to nurture your garden by consistently following these steps. Follow up is everything!

## Analyzing Potential Deals

There are many factors involved in analyzing a potential deal. These factors are critical, because in order to make a future profit, you must "buy the property right."

If you overpay for the property upfront, it will reduce your future chances of seeing a profit. The ideal time to make a future profit is when the property is initially purchased. This can only be achieved if all of the pertinent information concerning the subject property and competitive properties has been thoroughly gathered and analyzed.

This process involves extensive research into all areas of the property, including its construction, marketing, and financial aspects. Also, local market studies must be done to ensure investment timing is favorable. Only after this research and analysis will you be able to determine what you consider the true value of the property. You are buying an investment property to add value so understanding the current value will help you analyze the deal profit.

In analyzing the deal, you should contact any and all knowledgeable individuals who might be able to share insight on your questions. Some of these individuals will be extremely helpful, some at no charge, while others may charge for the information. The following may be good sources of information:

- Real estate agents
- City planning department
- Local police department
- Mortgage bankers
- General contractors
- Competitive property owners
- Property managers
- Consultants

Your goal is to understand the property and market in which you are investing. Is the market growing or contracting? What is the crime in the area? How does a subject property compare with its

competing properties on rents, amenities, class, sales values, etc.?
Can you find ways to create value to the subject property? Is the
subject property undervalued? Analyze the property and market
to uncover value so that you can better determine your profit
potential.

## Tips for Evaluating Property Location and Market Lifecycle

You should physically investigate a property's location, study the
area's past history, and research future growth prospects in the
local and regional markets. If the area has been run down, is it on
an upturn? Are future road changes going to affect the visibility
and accessibility to the property?

You should check with various sources to evaluate the
property's location:

- Get a police report on the area
- Get local demographics of the area (average incomes,
  unemployment rate, crime, etc.)
- Speak with real estate agents about local market
- Find out if companies are locating or leaving the area
- Look to see if you see new construction going on in the
  area
- Speak with local businesses to find sales activity
- Speak with local bankers
- Speak with other property owners
- Go down to the planning department to learn about the
  area
- Check the traffic counts in the area

One of the best things I have done is get into the middle of the
local market by walking the area. Park your car and walk around
to get a sense of the type of people and condition of the buildings
in the area. You will either get really excited about the
opportunity or you'll be scared off by the area. You'll be amazed
at what you find by walking, opening your eyes, listening, and
keeping your mind open.

*Market Life Cycle*

All real estate markets go through four stages of maturity. The four stages vary in length of duration. Some stages last 20 years while other can last over 50 years. Following are the four stages:

**Growing Market:** New building leads to growing areas that have newer construction, higher employment, lower crime, higher income levels, more active involvement in the community and a growing need by people to live, work and play in the area. These areas tend to have higher relative property values, lower cap rates and command higher rents.

**Declining Market:** As markets grow and land becomes less prevalent, new construction slows down. Properties become older with landscaping more mature. These markets were the former growing markets, and are typically found on the edges of the growing market. These areas tend to have Class A- to Class C+ buildings with lower rental rates. The demographics are weaker. People living and working in these areas are typically value people (affordable quality) who want the nicer lifestyle but can't afford the nicer areas.

**Stagnant Market:** Markets that are stagnant have no growth in population, jobs or energy. Little to no construction is occurring. This market has one of the lowest demographic profiles of the four stages. Low income and poverty is prevalent, crime is high, property vandalism is pervasive, and drug related activity is high. These markets have the lowest rents, lowest property values, highest delinquency problems, and highest tenant turnover. You must be a hands-on property owner in this market.

**Redeveloping Market:** After going through tough, stagnant times, these markets are rebounding into growing areas. Developers are venturing into these markets under urban renewal programs, many sponsored by local government. Properties in these areas typically are closer to central business districts where there is a concentration of employment. Property values are on the rise, rents are rising, and the overall market is getting stronger.

Understanding the local market and the life cycle stage it is in will help you decide if your property is located in a good location for your investment strategy. Don't ignore this important step in the investing process. If you do, you'll find many unexpected surprises on your door step down the road, costing you thousands.

## How to Assess Valuation Using the Capitalization Rate Method

Most people involved with income properties, whether investors or lender, use capitalization rates, aka cap rates, as an important gauge of valuations.

The capitalization rate is a ratio that is calculated by dividing the net operating income (the cash flow available after operating expenses is deducted from the total income) by the price of the property. Using this ratio, you must carefully and totally scrutinize the rent collection and expenses to make sure of an "apples to apples" comparison.

Cap rates are used widely in real estate because they provide a simple method to determine a percent return on investment. From that, investors can determine the proper pricing for an investment given an expected return. Thus, a cap rate is a rate of return on an investment assuming an all cash purchase.

For example, look at the Cap Rate Property Comparison chart on the next page. Notice the relationship between the Net Operating Income and the Sales Price on Properties A through C. If all three investments are offered for sale at the same price, $4,000,000, which property offers the best deal? Property C offers the best deal because the income (Net Operating Income) you would get on the $4,000,000 price is higher. The all-cash rate of return is 9.1% on a $4,000,000 investment.

Now let's look at it another way. In your local investment market, there is an average cap rate that is established by investors buying properties. The relationship between the Net

Operating Income (income) they are willing to accept at the price they pay is the cap rate.

For example, if the average cap rate in a local market for an apartment building is 7.6% , then you can calculate value of a property "for sale" by dividing the Net Operating Income (income from the investment) by the average cap rate (7.6%). In the Cap Rate Property Chart, take the Net Operating Income (NOI) for each property and divide it into the cap rate . Remember, the cap rate is a percentage so you'll need to move the decimal point. Take the NOI of Property A and divide it by the market cap rate of 7.6% ($303,600 divided by .076 = $3,994,737 or rounded off to $4,000,000).

Knowing the cap rate in your local market will allow you to value property by determining the NOI on a property "for sale." As you can see, it is critical to ensure you have accurate income and expense numbers when calculating the NOI.

What the current property owner or real estate broker represents as actual income and expenses may not be accurate. You should investigate all revenue and expense figures.  Many times the incomes may include money that is projected and is not currently being collected.  The expenses might not reflect costs that should be included or may include capital expenses.

| CAP RATE PROPERTY COMPARISON | | | |
|---|---|---|---|
| | Property A | Property B | Property C |
| Number of Units | 100 | 100 | 100 |
| One Bedroom Units | 100 | 50 | 0 |
| Two Bedroom | 0 | 50 | 100 |
| | | | |
| Average Rental Rate/ Mo. - 1x1 | $500 | $550 | $0 |
| Average Rental Rate/Mo. - 2x1 | $0 | $600 | $600 |
| Gross Rental Income | $600,000 | $660,000 | $720,000 |
| Other Income (2% of GRI) | $12,000 | $13,200 | $14,400 |
| Vacancy & Loss (10% of GRI) | -$60,000 | -$66,000 | -$72,000 |
| Total Income | $552,000 | $607,200 | $662,400 |
| Total Expenses (45% of GRI) | -$248,400 | -$273,240 | -$298,080 |
| | | | |
| Net Operating Income | $303,600 | $333,960 | $364,320 |
| | | | |
| Sales Price | $4,000,000 | $4,000,000 | $4,000,000 |
| | | | |
| Capitalization Rate | 7.6 | 8.4 | 9.1 |

*Value Add Example*

Let's say you buy Property A for $4,000,000 that is generating an NOI of $303,600. The owner has owned the property for over 10 years and hasn't put much money into keeping the property in good repair. As a result of the property being in poor condition, the rents are low compared to other rental properties in the local market.

You determine it will cost $100,000 to renovate the property so that it is in good repair and has good curb appeal. As a result, you are able to raise rents over the following three years. Let's say the new NOI would look like Property C - $364,320. Let's say the market cap rate over the three year period has stayed about the same – 7.6%. What would be the value of your apartment investment three years from now after renovations and stronger income from the rent increases?

We can figure the property valuation using the capitalization rate method by dividing the NOI by the cap rate. So in the scenario we have created, the new value would be....answer says? $4,800,000. ($364,320 divided by .076 = $4,793,684 or $4.8 million ). If an investor purchased the property for $4.8 million, they would generate $364,320 of NOI on that investment creating a 7.6% return.

## How to Value Property Using the Price per Square Foot Method

Using this measuring stick to determine value for an investment property can be valuable if you eliminate the noise in the final comparison.

The price per square foot method of assessing value is calculated by dividing the sales price by the total square footage. This method can be distorted due to the fact that investors measure square footage differently. Some investors use gross square footage while others use net square footage. Using an apartment property example, some units may include the square footage of balconies, patios, garages, basements, etc. into the total square footage. Make sure you are measuring similar square footages on the subject property against other comparable properties.

Let's take a look at two "identical" duplexes. The seller of Duplex A is claiming that his units have 1,000 square feet of space per unit, while the seller of Duplex B is claiming his units have 1,100 square feet per unit. Assuming a $100,000 asking price of Duplex A and $105,000 for Duplex B, it appears that Duplex A is selling for $50 a square foot, while Duplex B is selling for $47.73 a square foot.

The inexperienced investor would find out that Duplex B actually has 980 square feet per unit of rentable space after deducting the patio space (120 square feet of patio space deducted from 1,100 of total square footage per unit) from the total square feet. Thus, Duplex B is really selling for $53.57 per square foot on an "apples to apples" comparison basis. Assuming that all other factors were equal, Duplex A would be a better buy.

Be aware that analyzing the price per square foot for two similar properties will not always give you the complete picture you need to choose one over the other. Some multi-unit properties will have different mixes of unit size, and this will also throw off the price per square foot.

Another factor that should be considered when comparing properties is capital expenditures. If a property requires capital to renovate the property, make sure you add the cost of renovation to the asking price to get an adjusted asking price. Then use the adjusted asking price to calculate your new price per square foot (or price per unit).

Remember, you need to make sure when making comparisons that everything is an "apples to apples" comparison so that your valuations are correct. Go the extra mile to ensure you are getting all the facts before using your yardstick to determine value.

## Crunching the Numbers

When you get sales packages from real estate agents or sellers on properties for sale, you need to crunch the numbers. The information you get from any outside source should not be trusted. Let me say that again. Do not trust any income or expense information given to you from an outside source such as the seller or broker. Use their information as a basis, but you'll need to confirm the data given to you.

You will create your own operating pro forma (income and expense projection). There are many investment property software programs that will help you analyze a potential new acquisition. There are very advanced programs you can buy from Argus that cost $5,000 or there are more simple software programs from RealData.com that only cost $500. For most beginners and intermediate investors, this is a no-brainer; check out RealData.

Also, you can create your own investment analysis spreadsheet in Excel or some other spreadsheet software program. I had one created specifically for me that is unique to my situation.

Your pro forma will include a realistic income and expense projection on how you will operate the property. Be careful when projecting income and expense. Make sure you obtain local market data and use best practice methods when forecasting.

## Negotiating and Contracting for Purchase

You've come a long way. A good deal has been found, and it has been analyzed. The property return to the investors looks great, and there is a lot of money in it for you.
The decision is to go forward, and fast. But you do not want to do a lot of work and then have the deal dissolve before you can make any money. So what do you do? You tie up the property by putting it under contract.

When you are trying to lock up a property, you obviously want to end up with the best deal possible. So you negotiate with the seller to get the best deal possible. This may take some back and forth, but you want to be sure the seller is selling at a rock bottom price and/or on fabulous terms.

Once you have negotiated the best possible deal, you must solidify it in writing to protect yourself from doing a lot of work for nothing. The instrument you will use is a Letter of Intent (commonly referred to as "LOI") or a real estate purchase and sale agreement. An attorney should help draw up such document (or at least bless a standard industry contract). Your contract should build in plenty of safeguards (contingencies) so that you feel comfortable. The attorney's fees may be paid out of the funds you raise so that you don't have to use your own funds.

Make sure you build into your contract adequate time to perform tasks. Your contract should be structured to enable you to receive your earnest money deposit (tie up money) back should you decide not to go forward with the deal. You need time to conduct thorough due diligence, package the investment opportunity, raise funds, get financing, and close the deal. All these functions take time, so make sure you get enough.

Try to negotiate an extension of closing in your contract. Typically, you can exercise an option to extend the closing by paying an additional earnest money deposit. The time period you negotiate is very important for two reasons. One, it gives you an inexpensive extension to look at the property in more detail. A few thousand dollars for some additional time could save you many times the extension amount. Two, it allows you to package the investment properly and to raise the required funds. Because of these factors, you should always try to negotiate the longest escrow period possible.

When purchasing an income property, try for a minimum of 90 days, and take a 120 days or longer if you can get it. As a rule of thumb, I would never give myself less than 60 days for any property that I planned to syndicate. That is, from the time I tied up the property, I would want a minimum of 60 days before I had to come up with any additional funds. Get at least a 60-day closing with one or two extensions, conceivably creating 90-120 day closing period of time.

## Due Diligence and Inspection Prior to Purchase

When you put a property under contract that you are buying, you must inspect the property, market and financing. Completing the due diligence process takes a lot of time and effort. Due diligence can be out-sourced to companies that specialize in this type of work. Many times a property management company will do it for free if you give them the management of the property.

Here is a list of thirty due diligence areas to review. Every property will require additional due diligence review items but this list covers most areas.

**1. Property Measurement:** A survey should be conducted to determine the exact boundaries of the land area as well as the measurements of the gross and net rentable building (s). Make sure the square footage matches what the seller quoted you.

**2. Unit Mix:** Verify the unit mix by walking all the units. Compare the unit mix to other comparable properties and how the subject property fits into the market demand.

**3. Unit Size:** Verify the size of each space unit floor plan by measuring the square footage. Also, compare the space unit size to other comparable properties. Are the divided units bigger or smaller than the comps?

**4. Property Reputation:** Determine the current reputation of the property by speaking with local market participants.

**5. Curb Appeal:** First impressions are what sell. Review the condition of the property and how it fits into the overall market and other comps.

**6. Political Climate:** Familiarize yourself with local government attitudes and process.

**7. Community Services:** Determine if the property is located close to schooling, public transportation, and shopping. Community services are important to some tenants.

**8. Crimes Assessment:** Get a police report on the local market where the subject property is located. Also, speak with local crime officers whose beat covers the subject property. You'll be amazed at what you learn.

**9. Market Survey:** Conduct a detailed market survey to assess the competition. Learn what other properties are doing and how it may affect your operation.

**10. Tenant Profile:** Learn who the types of people or businesses are leasing at the subject property. Get demographic information, employment data, and credit worthiness data for property file.

**11. Sales Comps:** Research recent sale comps in your market. Real estate brokers have this information and will provide it if you ask.

**12. New Competition:** Analyze the local market and find out if new competitive rental properties are being built.

**13. Available Land for Development**: Properties located close to vacant land take on added risk of future development that brings new competition. Find out the zoning to determine if the vacant land is a threat.

**14. Construction Report:** Engage a professional building contractor or engineer to fully inspect the physical assets of the property. This will cost some money upfront but it will save you many times the cost of the report.

**15. Termite Report:** Engage a licensed pest control company to inspect the property for termites and dry rot, especially apartment properties.

**16. Interior Condition:** Walk each and every space unit and inspect the condition of the unit interiors. Assess the value of repairs needed in each unit.

**17. Interior and Exterior Design:** Design is critical to the success of a property. Contact tenants and leasing personnel to determine acceptability.

**18. Features and Amenities:** Check out the property and unit features and amenity package. How do they compare to the comps and are they needed in the marketplace?

**19. Personal Property:** Review the list of personal property transferring with the property. Check to see if there are any personal property taxes you need to account for in your pro forma.

**20. On-Site Availability:** Find out the zoning requirement, typically X number of parking spaces per X number of square footage or units. Too little parking will affect the property operation.

**21. Utilities:** Access to all necessary utilities is critical for the success of a property. You should confirm the vendor of each utility and who is responsible for paying each utility vendor.

**22. Permits and Licenses:** Get copies of all permits and licenses. Make sure they are current. Also, search planning and fire department records to see if there are any code violations.

**23. Real Estate Taxes:** Make sure you get the most recent tax bills (two years) and forecast in your operating pro forma and potential increases or decreases.

**24. Property Insurance:** Verify that insurance is available for the property. Get insurance loss run reports over the last five years if possible to see any insurance claims. Contact your insurance agent and get a quote for property insurance. Use this quote in your operating pro forma.

**25. Management Company:** Get information on the current management company and on-site staff. A list of on-site employees and their compensation will help you refine your pro forma.

**26. Title Insurance:** Order and review the title insurance commitment and schedules. Review these documents with your attorney.

**27. Operating Statements:** Get at least the last 24 months of operating history on the property. Look to see unusual expenses that may only apply to the current seller, higher than industry average expense and one-time expenses, capital expenses or anything that won't belong in your operating pro forma. Next, look at the income side of the operating statements to verify information supplied by the seller.

**28. Rent Roll:** Get a copy of the property rent roll with security deposits. Also get any other deposits the seller is liable for to the tenants.

**29. File and Lease Audit:** Inspect every lease thoroughly to verify rents and occupancy. Create a master lease abstract spreadsheet with each space number and add lease information such as lease expirations, rent rates, CAM, other charges and fees, unusual lease language, and so forth. Get a copy of their standard lease agreement and supporting exhibits and have them reviewed by a professional. Also, check the files for notices and work orders that may be an issue when you take over.

**30. Existing Mortgages**: Get copies of all existing mortgages and give them to your attorney for review. Make sure there are no surprises in the mortgage documents that negatively affect the financing you have agreed to with the seller.

## Financing and Closing the Transaction

After completing the due diligence on the property and removing some contract contingencies, it's time to line up your financing.

You will need to raise equity funds and to find a loan for the balance on the purchase price. During the escrow period, you may have been planning your money raising efforts, and in many cases, started to raise money from investors. If you've found a great deal, raising money should not be too tough. There is an entire money raising process, so I have dedicated the entire next chapter to how to raise equity funds.

## Getting Debt Financing

Ideally, getting financing from the existing lender is the quickest and cheapest approach. If you are able to assume a loan, obtain seller financing, or get restructured financing via a short sale, then the financing process is much easier and cheaper. I recommend using all efforts to go this route.

In the event you must get a new loan, you must start the process as soon as the property is put under contract to purchase. Engage a loan or mortgage broker to help you through the process. The broker will search the market to find you the very best loan. Having a broker will help you get the best loan and help you through the loan process.

## Items Lenders Will Require

Lenders look at property loans as an investment, albeit on the debt side. They approach the process similar to how you or an investor would look at the deal. Here are some items they will request:

- Business plan on the property
- Financial statements on the property
- Loan requirements
- Borrower resume and credentials
- Third party physical inspection reports
- Appraisal
- Source of equity funds
- Management company information

- Management and marketing plan
- Market survey
- Purchase and sale agreement

The process of getting a loan takes 30 to 60 days but typically gets done within 45 days. Make sure your purchase contract contains a financing contingency so that if you don't get the loan, your earnest money deposit gets returned. The cost of the loan ranges from .5% to 1%, depending on circumstances and loan type. The loan process can be overwhelming for some investors, so I highly recommending getting a mortgage broker to help you through the process.

### How Lenders Determine How Much Money to Lend on a Deal

While lenders will scrutinize the borrower and the market, they look at two important ratios to determine how much they will lend on an investment property.

Since a lender is loaning money based on the future income of the property, they want to make sure the income from the property will be able to support certain debt service payments. A lender will create a cash flow before debt service (aka Net Operating Income - NOI) forecast based on past and future income and expenses. Once a lender determines what they feel the NOI will be, they can determine how much money they will lend on the property.

A lender uses many metrics to determine loan amounts, but the two most important formulas they use are the debt service cover ratio (DSCR) and the loan to value ratio (LTV). Let's take a quick look at them both:

### Debt Service Coverage Ratio

The debt service coverage ratio is a formula that shows the lender how much coverage they have after all expenses and debt service are paid. The formula is as follows: Net Operating Income divided by Annual Debt Service = Debt Service Coverage Ratio.

For example, if a property has annual Net Operating Income of $100,000, and annual debt service of $80,000, then the debt service cover ratio is 1.25 ($100,000 / $80,000 = 1.25). This means that there is 25% coverage above the total expenses of the property.

## Loan to Value Ratio

This is the quickest and most common way to gauge the loan amount. This formula involves lending the maximum amount of money on the appraised value using a percentage of valuation. Many lenders use different percentages based on many criteria such as property location, borrower creditworthiness and stability, future potential, capital market conditions, etc.

If a lender is quoting they will lend 70% LTV, then they will lend a maximum of 70% of the appraised value. A property that has an appraised value of $1,000,000 will offer maximum loan proceeds of $700,000, which is 70% loan to value (LTV).

In the end, lenders establish how much to lend on a deal based on the predictability of future income the property will generate to cover debt service with a comfort factor. You can reasonably gauge the size of a loan by conservatively forecasting the NOI and applying a debt service coverage ratio quote by various lenders.

## Closing the Transaction

With all the pieces that go into getting your deal closed, you are now ready to close you deal. This is a very exciting time. A few days prior to closing, the title company and the closing attorneys start putting together the closing statement. The closing statement is a worksheet that shows all the charges and credits for the buyer and seller. The statement will include prorations for rents, security deposits, mortgage interest, and property taxes. All property operating expenses are handled outside escrow because many times the buyer may want to keep services, including utility. In some instances, the title company will handle property operating expenses, but normally this is handled outside of the closing.

A couple of days prior to closing, the buyer will sign the loan documents and closing documents. The seller will sign closing documents, including delivering a signed deed transferring the property. When everything is in to the title company, they will compute how much the buyer needs to close the transaction.

The day of closing, the buyer will wire transfer the equity funds and the lender will wire transfer the debt funds. The property transfer is recorded at the county recorder and then the closing is official. The title company will send checks to all parties owed money, including the seller sale proceeds. The buyer gets the ownership deed and the seller gets the cash.

# Lessons Learned from Over 40 Years of Real Estate Value Investing – Straight From the Gut

Steven Fogel, investor, author, comedian and artist, shares with us lots of great ideas, funny stories and tons of wisdom on lessons learned from over 40 years of real estate value investing. Steve built his company into one of the largest owner-operators of retail properties in the nation with a portfolio of approximately 100 properties in 23 metropolitan markets valued at over $1.5 billion.

Steve started as a real estate entrepreneur at the young age of 20 buying small apartment buildings in the greater Los Angeles area. In the 1980's, he wrote a bestselling book entitled, *The Yes-I-Can Guide to Mastering Real Estate.* In this interview, Steve shares brutally candid real life experiences on lessons he learned over his long career - Straight from the gut!

**You capitalize on undervalued opportunities. How'd you get started?**

I got started because as a kid, my mother was a widow, and I was 12 when my dad passed away. She made her living doing real estate. In '54, in California, people kept migrating to California, and so no matter what house you bought, you could buy a house, make a couple of bucks, and move on to another house. My mother did this, and I remember as a child moving a lot. She had an eight-unit apartment house, and by the time I was 18, she had gotten into her own part of life where it came up that I took over an 8-unit apartment house, and ultimately made two or three other little apartment houses on it. I became a wheeler-dealer from that point forward in real estate. Were I to have had better grades in school and better guidance, I probably could have gotten into a good law school, and then I'd be an attorney. But the only law school I could get into was beneath my personal false pride level, so I messed around with whatever was easy – and I had no family business to go into and no profession. So I just kept doing the real estate stuff.

**With all your wisdom, looking back over your career, are there three or four pieces of advice that you would give to value investors?**

The main advice I've given in this lifetime is, "Don't eat the yellow snow." There just plain are no words of wisdom – the only thing I know now that I didn't know then is nothing works without integrity. So you will never have anything work for you in your life in any way unless you have your personal integrity intact, and eventually, it'll fall apart and bite you on the ass. There are two things you need to do: (1) you need to tell the truth, particularly to yourself (2) and you need to keep your agreements. And again, it's agreements particularly with your self. And if you tell the truth, and if you keep your agreements, life will work just fine for you.

When it comes to the real estate stuff, what you have to do is see value. And seeing value, in the context that I mean it, is you have to have enough experience – and you load yourself up by asking questions and looking and being curious and being diligent – until you really find out that, hey, I've talked to 1,000 people, everybody agrees this particular piece of property in general is worth, give or take, this much, and if I can buy it for less than that much, I see the value in it. So one way or another, we keep loading ourselves to see value, and when you can see value – when you innately, inside yourself, know – then that's really the key.

**You were very heavy into apartments, early on, and then you changed to shopping centers. Why the change?**

This was in 1978. There were a couple of reasons. The main reason was that rent control was coming along. There was a lot of talk about it, and the thought of rent control was frightening. At the same time, we were in a business environment where the world agreed that apartments would sell for a premium, so regardless of what you – like today, if you want to buy an apartment, it's very improbable that anybody buying an apartment house at fair market value today will really make a cash flow on it early on. And the reason for that is because the world says that we will pay a premium for an apartment house, so whereas, you could put the same money in a bond, you'll get like a 4 or 5% return. You put it in a REIT, you'll get this or that return. But the apartment house, you get a smaller return. Does that make sense, what I'm saying?

**Yeah, the cap rates are lower on apartments, for sure.**

Yeah. So we could transfer the money from the apartments, where they were selling at a premium. We get a premium amount of money for it, and there were other forms of real estate at the time which were in the commercial properties, the mini-malls and stuff like that, where we could sell an apartment, where we were getting, based on the actual value – the equity we had in the apartment, at the time of sale. We may only be getting 2 or 3% on our equity. We could take the same capital, put it into a mini-mall, where the rules of the game were you could get a 10% cash on cash return because they were selling at a discount. So we took the money, because we were afraid of the environment for rent control, and we got out of that (apartments) and transferred them into the commercial properties, where we got a premium. So that's why we did it.

Do you know the Zen story that ends up "and then we shall see?" It's a very famous story. It's probably three, four, five hundred years old. China warlord gives his son a horse. The son's maybe 12, 14 years old, and all the village people say, "Wow, look at that lucky kid to get a horse." And they go to the Zen master, and they say, "Isn't that a lucky kid to get a horse?" And the Zen master says, "And we shall see." And then, about a year later, the kid falls off the horse and breaks his arm. And they all go to the Zen master and say, "Isn't it terrible that that kid had the horse?" And the Zen master says, "And we shall see." And then, about a year later, they're constricting the emperor for service, and the emperor's army – all of the young people, and they don't take the kid because his arm's messed up. And they say to him, "Isn't he a lucky kid that he doesn't have to go. . .?" "And we shall see."

You're asking me today about trading the apartments for the commercial in the '70s. That was a really good thing. If I would have asked the Zen master, "Is this the answer?" He would have said, "And we shall see."

If I would have left the same money in the same apartments, probably be worth the same or more without doing any of the things I did between then and now because they are still selling for a premium. So all of the things you're saying, if you take a snapshot, they're very clever. But you know, you go and "we shall see" period of time later, and they turn out to be stupid. And then you wait awhile more, and it – Nixon was a bad guy; he was a good guy; he was a bad guy; he's a good guy. You know, I may not be answering these questions in your usual way – in the way your expectation is, but it makes no difference to me.

## Does every property have a story?

Every property does have a story. It's your job to find out whether the story is accurate or not, and it's your job to find out if that's the real story, what other stories are there. One of the things that is a basic principle is when the tide goes up, all the ships go up, and when the tide goes down, all the ships go down.

So if the story is always bad management. Well, that's just a story. You have to find out, is it really true or not? The story I have seen literally thousands of tenants where I have walked the property prior to buying it, and you ask these tenants how is your store doing? So what you have to do is dig, dig, dig 'til you get as close to the source as you can. So what you're trying to do, is you're trying to find out, is the story the real problem? It probably is the real problem that the supply and demand aren't together, and it may be location, location, location.

**Brokers typically say that it's just bad management if you're a buyer. But is it really bad management?**

The question is, is it really bad management? And then the question under that is, could you do any better?

**Why do you manage your own properties?**

The point of view I have always had about third party managers is the property management business is a terrible business. I compare it to the travel agency business. If you do everything you're supposed to do, you deliver to your customers what was expected, life is never going to go right, so it's always going to be a problem. So there's always going to be a problem for the property manager.

By the way, it's now 40 years I've been doing this. People say they're a really great property management company, but in general, you also ask if a property has a story. Almost all the story is bad management. I can tell you that probably in the last four or five years, we've probably bought 20 or 30 shopping centers where major property managers were managing them. And it's always the story - bad management. They have other fish to fry.

I don't think that there is any property management where there is someone high enough up on the food chain that really cares, that really would be responsible.

**How are you capitalizing on today's distressed real estate market?**

We are an organization who is constantly looking for all of the properties that fit our operating principles. Our operating principles are currently retail. Is that the best operating principle? No. If we would've switched back to apartments, 15 years ago, we probably would have made a lot more money than we made in the commercial. But you get used to doing something.

You know the story of the scorpion and the frog? Oh, it's one of the best stories of all time. The scorpions and frogs are not good together. The scorpion lives on this side of the stream and says, "My wife is on the other side; I've got to get there, but I don't know how to swim." He sees a frog and says to the frog, "Will you swim me over to the other side?" The frog says, "No, I'm not going to do that because scorpions kill frogs." And the scorpion says, "Well, often we do, but on this particular time, all I want to do is go across there for my girlfriend. If I kill you, we'd both drown." Frog says, "Okay. I get it. I'll take you over there." Halfway across the stream, the fangs of the scorpion go into the frog's back, and the frog says, "Well, why did you do that?" And the scorpion says, "Because that's my nature." We're buying commercial properties, which we've always bought, because that's our nature.

## Retail properties are great investments.

"We shall see."

**Steven Jay Fogel**
Co-Founder, Westwood Financial

After 40 years as a real estate entrepreneur buying deals, Steve has built his company into one of the largest owner-operators of retail properties in the nation with a portfolio of approximately 100 properties in 23 metropolitan markets valued at over $1.5 billion. In the 1980's he wrote a bestselling book entitled, *The Yes-I-Can Guide to Mastering Real Estate.* Recently, Steve wrote a book entitled, *My Mind Is Not Always My Friend,* which offers readers lessons on how to mentally become stronger personally and professionally.

The Inside Game To Real Estate Investing

# Chapter 8

## How to Find Partners to Fund Your Deals

*"We actually bought a condominium in Las Vegas on Las Vegas Boulevard. We're thinking, 'Oh, this is awful.' And our sponsor said, "Trust us; this is what we do every day." And we did. A month and a half later, we bought a condo for $250,000.00, and sold it for $850,000."*

> Rory Maguire
> Realty Capital Partners

Did you find a great deal? If you can't factually support a great deal to your potential investors, then it will be hard to raise money. It's the most critical thing you need in your arsenal when approaching investors for money. However, because you are a Value Hound, this shouldn't be a problem because the number one rule of real estate value investing is to never lose money, so we have to buy with a margin of safety to preserve capital by paying $.50 for $1.00. You found that great deal, right? Fantastic!

Now that you have this great deal, it's time to spread the word by communicating with potential investors. I will walk you through the process step-by-step, from beginning to end. Raising money is a process and it gets easier every time you do a deal because you are planting seeds with potential investors. Some investors may not invest in your first deal, but will invest on other deals. The best source of future equity is from your existing investors. Happy investors want to invest more, and the best part, they spread the word and bring in other investors. It's like a snow ball going downhill; the longer it goes down the hill, the bigger the snow ball gets. I want to help you start the snow ball down the hill.

## Inside Look at Using Other People's Money

If you are like many investors without enough capital to purchase commercial real estate, then you have been researching the subject of Other People's Money, or commonly known as "OPM." In the group investment process, a group sponsor (you) raises "equity" capital for the group investment using OPM. When you raise money for your investment, you are creating a group investment know as a syndication. You are called the syndicator or sponsor of the group investment.

One of the primary reasons many people are hesitant to invest in commercial real estate is because property values are often so high that it takes a great deal of money to complete a transaction, even when obtaining a 70% to 80% loan.

There are few people who have the financial resources needed to purchase a $5 million building. However, group sponsored investments offer a vehicle for sponsors and syndicators to purchase larger commercial properties. By pooling funds together from investors using OPM, a group investment can be organized to purchase large commercial properties. Most of the largest investors in the world create group investments to buy commercial real estate. I am going to show you the inside secrets to how they form group investments in this chapter.

## The Power of Small Investment Groups

Why should a small investment group be able to do better than an individual buyer? Simple, when you stop to look at it. There are three critical reasons why small investment groups fare better in the marketplace.

Here's the way I look at it. The main problem is that there are more buyers than sellers at the bottom of the heap. Oh sure, the market is glutted with properties for sale, but that's because the sellers can be counted. There is no way to count the buyers. So take my word for it, they are out there with "a few bucks and a sharp pencil," and as a result, the law of supply and demand works to increase prices on those less costly properties, without accompanying gains in actual value.

Money is always a "scarce commodity." So, with nothing down, EVERYONE becomes a buyer. But, like a poker game, raise the ante and you begin to chase people out of the pot. As the down payments and purchase prices increase the cost of "staying in the game," you quickly begin to narrow the number of players – and by doing so you LESSEN the COMPETITION.

By using groups of investors and combining their small individual investments – with the synergistic magic of the joint venture or partnership enterprise – you can move up into an echelon of higher property values where competition is far less severe. In that rarified atmosphere, the real "bargains" abound – due to economy of scale – and with your new financial clout, outstanding profits can be made. This market niche, as I call it, lies between $1,000,000 and $5,000,000 in sales price - just below the institutional players but above individuals.

Small group investments will do better than individuals because there is less competition of buyers at higher prices, better economy of scale from higher intrinsic value, and better synergism from a group than with individuals going their separate ways.

## Understanding the Basic Group Investment Structure

Let's talk about some definitions and terminology used in this business so we are communicating in the same language. Understanding the entity structure is important to properly organizing your entity.

Let's first understand that the term "syndication or joint venture" simply means organizing GROUP INVESTMENTS. And a group investment is two or more people joined together in a common enterprise usually involving "risk capital" for the purpose of conserving their equity investment and making a profit. While there are many vehicles for group investments (limited partnerships were popular in the 80's), we are going to be concerned here with only one main type of partnership – "limited liability companies."

A limited liability company, commonly called an "LLC," is a business structure that combines the pass-through taxation of a partnership or sole proprietorship with the limited liability of a corporation. The LLC really is a limited partnership combined with a corporation – the best of both worlds.

Like owners of partnerships or sole proprietorships, LLC owners report business profits or losses on their personal income tax returns; the LLC itself is not a separate taxable entity. Like owners of a corporation, however, all LLC owners are protected from personal liability for business debts and claims -- a feature known as "limited liability." This means that if the business owes money or faces a lawsuit, only the assets of the business itself are at risk. Creditors usually can't reach the personal assets of the LLC owners, such as a house or car. (Both LLC owners and corporate shareholders can lose this protection by acting illegally, unethically, or irresponsibly.)

For these reasons, many people say the LLC combines the best features of the partnership and corporate business structures.

## Who is the Sponsor?

The sponsor is the group investment organizer. The sponsor can be an individual or an entity that lawfully pools together investors or partners for the purposes of making an equity investment into an LLC entity.

The sponsor is totally responsible for the entire investment process from beginning to end. The sponsor finds and evaluates the investment, arranges the financing, organizes the investors, closes the deal, manages the day-to-day partnership business, eventually sells the investment, and then disburses the profits to the LLC members. For the sponsor's efforts, he or she is paid various fees and receives a percentage of the profits.

## How is the LLC Organized?

The LLC is organized to hold title to the real estate investment. The sponsor finds partners who invest in the LLC as members. The LLC is comprised of members that own an interest in the LLC. The LLC will own the property with the entity name held on title.

Partners do not hold title to LLC property in their own names. They hold a piece of paper (membership interest in the LLC) that describes their interest in the LLC entity. This is no different than a corporation holding its plant and fixtures in the corporate name, with its stockholders owning an interest represented by the paper stock certificates of the company.

The LLC can be set up to be managed as MANAGER managed or MEMBER managed. Typically, the sponsor controls the LLC so the LLC is set up to be manager managed. On smaller LLC's with few partners or relatively new sponsors without a track record, the partners may want more control and request the LLC to be member managed, allowing them to be involved with on-going decisions. The way you investment LLC is managed may be a negotiating point for you with your partners.

## Duties of the Syndicator

Obviously, one of the most important requirements for purchasing commercial property is having enough money to complete the transaction. You will be forming a group of people to pool together enough capital to let you close a particular transaction. They, the investors, get a portion of the income and appreciation for their funds. You, the syndicator, get the rest for finding, analyzing, purchasing, and managing the property.

When you decide to form investor groups, you run into a situation where the law may require you to take on a specific duty to fully inform your co-investors of all aspects of the property and the investment. Most people getting involved in group investments are usually under-informed or inexperienced with regard to the following group-investment concepts:

- The legal aspects of the co-ownership of real estate
- Factors that affect the value of commercial real estate
- The process and responsibilities involved in property management
- The fair compensation to the group manager or "syndicator"

When you take on the role of syndicator, you actually create an "agency duty" to your co-investors. You have a higher responsibility to disclose all of the aspects that can affect a particular property investment, both good and bad. So when you form a group for investment, it's very helpful to have a checklist for all of the things you need to do so that you meet your duties and responsibilities to your partners and investors.

## How Group Sponsors Get Paid and the Types of Fees They Can Earn

There are many various types of fees that group sponsors get paid for organizing and operating a group investment. Check out the fees that sponsors pay themselves from the investment group funds on behalf of the partnership.

Before I list the types of fees sponsors get paid, let's review the cash items from a hypothetical business plan to capitalize the investment group. Sponsors create a business plan for the property investment that has the "sources and uses of funds" required to operate the real estate property business. Here is a sample of possible items in the "sources and uses" of a business plan:

- Cash down payment to the seller of the property
- Escrow and Closing costs
- Professional fees (legal, financial, money raiser)
- Loan fees
- Appraisal fee
- Property Inspection Fees
- Property Insurance

- Renovation or capital improvement funds
- Cash reserves for the partnership
- Negative cash flow "carry reserve"
- Sponsor Fees

The sources and uses will vary depending on your specific transaction. I've only given you possible items to consider when putting together your business plan.

A sponsor raises the total "sources and uses" funds in a partnership or joint venture entity. These funds are held in a partnership bank account that the sponsor normally controls. When escrow closes, the sponsor disburses funds to close the deal, pays himself his fees and keeps the remaining funds in a partnership to run the new entity.

**Types of Fees Sponsors Can Earn**

Here are the types of fees sponsors can earn for their efforts. These fees are fully disclosed in the investor offering memorandum, and sometimes, are negotiated with investors. To get paid, sponsors simply write a check for the fee due from the partnership bank account to themselves.

These fees are only examples of the types of fees sponsors roll into their investments. Fees are paid for services rendered. Do not add fees to you investments unless they are warranted, justified and agreed to by your investor(s). Any fess taken by a sponsor should take a back seat to the performance of the investment.

**1. Acquisition Fee.** This upfront fee is paid by the new buying partnership entity for finding, analyzing, evaluating, financing, and closing the property investment. Acquisition fees range from . 5% to 3% of the purchase price, depending on the size of the deal.

**2. Real Estate Commission.** If you act as a broker in the transaction for the partnership (you must be licensed), you can get paid a fee from the seller of the property. Typical commissions range from 3-6% of the sales prices. Normally, the sponsor can only receive one fee – either an acquisition fee or a real estate commission.

**3. Organization or Underwriting Fee.** This upfront fee is paid by the partnership for putting together the group investment. The fees range from 3% to 10% of the total money raised. Again, it depends on the amount of money raised.

**4. Construction Management Fee.** This on-going fee is paid from construction money for capital improvements. This fee ranges from 5% to 10% of the renovation funds held for construction of the property.

**5. Asset Management Fee.** This on-going annual fee is paid from the property operations, typically below the NOI under partnership expenses, for property oversight. Fees range from . 25% to 1% of the asset value depending on asset size with the lower rate on bigger properties.

**6. Partnership Management Fee.** This on-going fee is paid like the asset management fee with similar fee ranges. Typically, both fees are not paid. The fee is structured around the arrangement with its investors.

**7. Property Management Fee.** This on-going fee is paid from the operations of the property on a monthly basis. Fees range from 3%-6% of the total monthly collected revenues of the property.

**8. Accounting and Tax Fees.** These event specific fees are paid for accounting and tax related services on behalf of the property and partnership. Fees range from $30-$100 per hour.

**9. Refinancing Fee.** There is a lot of effort that goes into getting a loan. To compensate the Sponsor for these efforts, a fee is paid at closing on the loan of .5%-1% of the total loan amount.

**10. Resale Commission.** This fee is paid on the future sale of the property to a licensed real estate broker. The sponsor is the listing broker and cooperates with an outside, arms length, selling broker where they split the commission. If the sponsor is not licensed, the partnership can pay an advisory fee on the sale. The real estate commission is the prevailing industry rate.

In addition to the above fees, sponsors typically are reimbursed from the partnership for out-of-pocket expenses, and any other reasonable items agreed to in the partnership agreement.

Every group investment partnership will vary on the type of fees the sponsor can earn. This list of ten types of fees I mentioned is only to show the different types of possible fees so that you can structure your deals more appropriately. I can't emphasize this enough: don't take fees unless you are adding value to the process. Larger investors will typically allow only a few agreed upon fees. Don't overload the partnership with excessive fees because it has to earn a reasonable rate of return, as outlined in the investor offering memorandum.

In addition to earning fees, group sponsors and syndicators earn backend performance profits. Let's take a look at how partnerships can be structured.

## Structuring the Profits in Your Syndication

Since all investors are making an economic decision when they invest in real estate, they will carefully analyze how much money they will invest and how they will get their original investment back with profits.

Profits are split between the investors and the sponsor based on a schedule of priority. The first money returned from the net sale proceeds of the property are the investors' (and sponsor if they invested) invested capital; the money invested in the deal. Next, investors receive a preferred return on their investment funds, typically 7-10% per year. Once the investors have gotten their investment back plus a preferred return, the remaining profits are split between the investors and sponsor based on the original agreement.

*Cash Flow*

The cash flow that the property generates will be available to distribute to the investors. There are many ways that the cash flow can be split among the partners. One way is to split this cash equally between investors and the sponsor; another is to allocate to investors 100% (or whatever percentage that fits your deal) of the cash flow until they receive their preferred return. Any cash available over that amount can then be split. A common arrangement at this point, splits the available cash flow by allocating in accordance with the backend profit split percentages (i.e.: 75% to investors and 25% to the sponsor).

*Refinancing Proceeds*

Upon the refinancing of the property, new funds could be generated either by increased cash flow or from tax-free dollars from the difference between the old and new mortgages. These funds could then be available to fund any renovation work, to fund the working capital account, or to distribute to the partners. If the decision is made to distribute this cash, the deal could be structured to give these proceeds back to the investors as a return of their initial capital, or they could be split between the investors and the sponsor.

*Resale Proceeds*

When the resale occurs, the deal is coming to a close. Typically, the deal is structured one of two ways. In the first, the investors receive the remaining dollars due from their original investment, plus any dollars due from their preferred cash flow agreement. The remaining cash would then be split between the investors and the sponsor. This split can be equal or 75 percent to 25 percent with increases to the sponsor based upon certain predetermined formulas. The second method used could be to split the profits 90 percent to 10 percent with increases to the sponsor upon a specific formula based upon hitting certain benchmarks.

**7 Big Reasons Why Investors are Attracted to Group Investments**

To better position your investment opportunity to investors, you need to understand why investors are attracted to group investments. Take a look at the benefits investors enjoy with group investments.

**1. Specialized and Experienced Group Managers.** The group manager provides the expertise in locating great investment opportunities, negotiating good financing, over-seeing the property operations, and insuring the business plan is effectively executed. Co-Investors do not have the burden or hassle of the enterprise.

**2. Economies of Scale.** A group of Co-Investors have more purchasing power than an individual, thus creating a better opportunity to purchase a property at a discount.

**3. Market Price Niche Investing.** Opportunities to purchase great deals exist within a narrowly defined target group. The best price range to get a great deal exists at a price just above what a typical individual investor could afford, and a price just below what a large institutional investor would pay. In today's market, that price range is between $1 million and $5 million.

**4. Security in Numbers.** The investment risk is spread among many small Co-Investors so that any unforeseen "bumps in the road" are less severe on the group than the impact would be on one person alone.

**5. Exclusive Group.** Each Co-Investor is a member of a relatively exclusive group. The group manager only selects those Co-Investors who have similar investment goals and philosophies as herein mentioned.

**6. Limited Liability.** The Co-Investor enjoys limited liability just like that benefiting corporate stockholders.

**7.  Peace of Mind.**  No management headaches or responsibilities on the part of the Co-Investor.  The Co-Investor is completely passive with none of the burden or concerns of management.

These are the primary reasons and benefits desired by investors. There are undoubtedly other cogent reasons why investors like group investments, such as the property or management may be local, diversity of their investments, or the pride of ownership the investor feels in owning an investment property.

There is any number of reasons motivating investors to make investments into group investments – the list could go on. Here's a reason why to invest that I bet motivates some investors - MAKE MONEY.

## The Basic Syndication Road Map

Every syndication follows its own path but this basic eight step process will get you around the track and on the correct path to creating successful group investments. Keep in mind that each of the eight steps on the road map offers its own area of specialty.

Syndication is the use of other people's money through pooling of their money.  More specifically, syndication is the uniting of two or more persons (or entities) in an association, under central management, to carry out a particular transaction for profit.

As a syndicator (typically referred to as a Sponsor), you create, analyze and structure the investment opportunity, package the investment documents, raise the funds, organize and manage the investment, and share in the profits and other benefits of full involvement.

You could perform all of the sponsor functions, or you could do some of them and hire out the other ones.  You might only handle the real estate investment functions such as finding, evaluating, financing, closing and managing the investment.  On the money raising side, you might hire out these functions such as organizing the investment vehicle, packaging investment partnership documents, and raising the required funds.  For new sponsors, you will likely be handling all the functions.

*Basic Road Map*

These are the complete eight steps from beginning to end of the syndication process. Each step involves its own specialty and requires some knowledge and expertise to carry out.

1. Find an investment opportunity
2. Analyze and evaluate the property
3. Tie up the property – Put it under contract
4. Package the opportunity
5. Raise funds from investors
6. Close the deal
7. Manage the partnership asset(s)
8. Sell the property and disburse profits

While this process might seem daunting, it is quite simple once you have been around the track and have seen the scenery. All new syndicators should start on smaller deals so that they can see the entire track. Once you understand each function, especially the first five steps from finding a deal to closing it, you can start doing bigger deals.

There really is no limit to the size of a deal you can syndicate. If you want to keep your investment groups small, that's OK. If you want to graduate to bigger deals, that's OK too. If you look around at some of the biggest properties in your city, you might find it interesting to learn that most of those deals were syndicated using the same basic road map.

## 20-Step Syndication Process From Beginning to End

Get a big picture of what the syndication process looks like from beginning to end. See how the syndication process evolves over its full life span. This will help you better plan and make smarter decisions.

1. Research and find an available rental property in a particular submarket and choose a property to purchase.

2. Prepare preliminary analysis of the property investment. This would include the properties financial history, the physical conditions of the property, the local submarket, rent comps and sale comps. From your investment analysis, determine the property valuation and your offer price.

3. Create a letter of intent (LOI) or purchase contract. Make an offer and negotiate the deal to tie up the property and get control of it. You must have the property under contract before beginning your fund raising efforts.

4. Open escrow with your contract. Order third party reports and title report.

5. Conduct a detailed and thorough due diligence. Complete an analysis of the seller's actual income and expenses, investigate the physical condition of the property, review leases, investigate the property operations, and study the title report. In this step, you are investigating the property to ensure there are no future surprises and it supports your business plan objectives.

6. Engage a loan broker to find and secure competitive debt financing. If financing is assumable, then contact the lending group to begin the loan assumption process.

7. Form the new group investment entity. Begin the legal process of setting up the group investment. I highly recommend the assistance with your attorney and accountant.

8. Prepare the Investment Circular (Private Placement Memorandum), Subscription Agreement, Articles of Organization and Operating Agreement for the group investment LLC.

9. Market the Investment Circular to potential investors to fund your purchase.

10. Pool together the investors. Once you have approved the investor's suitability, you need to get their signatures on the

Subscription Agreement and the Operating Agreement of the LLC. You'll also want to deliver their funds to escrow for the close.

11. When the required investment group funds have been raised, the Syndicator begins to close the deal.

12. The Syndicator now files the Articles of Organization with the state in which the LLC is formed.

13. The Syndicator now assigns his right to purchase the property to the LLC in an amendment to escrow prior to the close. The property now vests in the name of the LLC and the Syndicator gets his ownership percentage in the LLC.

14. The purchaser closing funds (down payment, fees and closing costs) for the transaction are paid to the seller from the LLC member's contributions.

15. The property closes escrow and the group investment LLC takes possession of the property.

16. The Syndicator now sends copies of the closing documents to all of the members of the LLC, along with any other organizational documents that may not already be in their possession.

17. The Syndicator now steps into the role of the partnership manager. The Syndicator oversees the property on behalf of the group investment LLC, executing the business plan.

18. Distribution of cash flow is delivered to all the investors on regular periodic periods. Also, regular partnership reporting and communications are sent to investors.

19. Meetings are held to inform and update investors on the status and progress of the investment property. At times, the investors may make major decisions, such as add or replace investors, refinance, or sell the property.

20. When it's finally time to sell the property, the Syndicator manages that process including:

- Hiring a real estate broker or representing the LLC himself to sell the property
- Negotiating purchase offers and coordinating closing proceedings
- Providing disclosures and reports during the closing
- Making final profit distributions to investors
- Winding down and terminating the investment group partnership LLC

## Where to Look for Equity Investors

Once the amount of equity is determined, the sponsor starts making his list of personal equity investors. This list outlines some of the best places to find investors for your deals.

- Friends & Family
- Business associates
- Broker dealers who specialize in real estate
- Accountants who have clients who want to invest in real estate
- Financial planners who have clients who want to invest in real estate
- Attorneys who have clients who want to invest in real estate
- Real estate agents who know potential investors
- Bankers who have clients who might be potential investors
- Insurance agents who have wealthy clients
- Real estate investment companies
- Past investors in other deals
- Property owners who invest in real estate

This list will give you a starting point as you sit down to make your list of potential investors. Make sure to ask the people on your list if they know of anyone else that might be potential investors in your deal. You'll be amazed at how many investors are referred.

## How to Find and Close Investors Using These 6-Steps

The most common question asked by syndicators is, "How do you find investors?" Unless you have already been syndicating, people generally show some awed respect for this seemingly impossible task. In fact, actually doing it is not as mysterious or as difficult as you might imagine, although it does require some organization and concentration.

Before we get started, I must remind you that selling membership interest in an LLC to other investors is a security that requires following state and federal guidelines. In the selling process, you must follow some guidelines because you will be making a private offering. Each state has its own guidelines so make sure you review them. One common theme among state and federal security laws is that the person (potential investors) must be a personal contact.

## Step 1 – Develop a First Stage List

Whether this is your first or tenth venture, you start the process out the same way. As such, you have friends, relatives, clients, customers, or some close business or work associates. Put their names down on a list. You should have no trouble assembling 25 to 50 qualified names. If you are in the real estate business, such as a real estate agent, you probably know many other real estate investors to add to your list.

## Step 2 – Contact Those on the List

Although you eventually should try to meet with the potential investor, your initial communication can be by telephone. After opening with pleasantries, let the potential investor know that you are involved in something that is "unique," or that "offers an unusual opportunity," or that "looks to be extremely profitable for me, and I can get you in on it if it makes sense to you, too." In other words, you want to hook your contact right up front. You want to use some catchy word or phrase that piques their interest so that, hopefully, they will ask you to tell them more.

## Step 3 – Get the Private Placement Memorandum (PPM) in the Potential Investors Hands

Ideally, you will meet with prospective investors for a few minutes to hand them the package along with a brief cover letter. Your letter highlights the main points (the property, income and value benefits, timing, investment amount, etc.). These are all extracted from the PPM package; they are just highlighted in the letter. The cover letter is a highly effective sales tool.

## Step 4 – Develop a Second Stage List and Get the PPM to those on the List

After completely going through the first list, you will know how many of those potential investors are good prospects for your deal. If you don't feel that you can fund your deal solely with the people on the first list, then put together a second stage list while sending out packages to the first list.

The second list requires some deeper thought. You'll be amazed at how many additional names you'll come up with after sitting down for an hour with a piece of paper and pencil. To stimulate your thinking, list various categories of businesses, professionals, organizations and other people you know in these categories. This list might contain your tax accountant, financial advisor, attorney, doctor, church member, social group member, teacher or other people you know. Soon, you'll find you have another list of 25-50 people.

So that you stay organized, add these names to your first list. You always want to have a master list from which to work from. Your selling efforts are exactly the same as on the first list.

## Step 5 – Develop a Third Stage List and Make Contact with These People

You may not need to go this far. You should have funded your group investment partnership with investors from the first two groups. However, if you still need additional investors, the concentration with pencil and paper as used before will produce more prospects for your deal.

Go through all the categories noted above to ferret out new names previously missed. Also, your friends and investors that have agreed to invest money with you can be sources of prospects for you. While you do not want to enlist them as "finders" of potential investors, their knowledge of your deal can result in some of their friends being added to you third stage list.

## Step 6 – Close Your Prospects into the Deal

You will, of course, be signing people up and collecting their funds throughout this whole time period. As you are doing so, you must make sure that they qualify for the deal. Don't be afraid to tell them that they just don't qualify (too little income/net worth, lack of understanding, etc.). It is much better to lose them now as an investor than to get them in and have them pressed financially if the deal does not work as planned. Also, they may be a future prospect and will hold you in high regard.

If the prospect is qualified, have them complete and sign the Statement of Suitability and its Questionnaire exhibit(s). This statement, the signed LLC operating agreement and their check constitute the documents you need to have them in the deal.

There you go. You have a 6-step system to raise money for your small group investment property. The first deal is the hardest, but once you get it done, each subsequent deal gets easier. You'll find current investors referring other investors and soon you'll have more money to invest than good deals.

Finally, make sure you have a great deal before trying to raise money. Great deals are always easier to find investors for. Make your raising money job easier by bringing great deals to your potential investors.

## How to Use Split Funding to Get Your Deal Closed

This special technique will help you get your deal closed using fewer funds while increasing your leverage without any cost. Use this technique during negotiations. Figuring out how to this technique will help you buy good deals.

With the split funding technique, you agree to pay the requested down payment, but you don't pay it all at once. In reality, all you do is establish a payment plan in which you make two or MORE payments. The down payment then is viewed as a separate event from the payment of the rest of the purchase price.

For example, you have offered Dave, a seller of a small apartment building you want to buy, a purchase price of $1,150,000. The terms of your offer consist of a $150,000 down payment with the assumption of the existing first mortgage of $800,000. Dave will hold a second mortgage for the balance of his equity of $200,000 for 7-years at 8% annual interest.

Dave objects to the low down payment and high second mortgage. He insists on $250,000 down payment.

You think about why you like this deal. This property offers the opportunity to add value over the next couple of years. With better management and a few renovations, you can raise rents and increase the value by $500,000. But, you don't have the extra $100,000 down payment the seller is requesting. So, you offer a split funding to the seller.

Using the split funding technique, you would meet his request with a positive statement – "Okay Dave, I'll pay the $1,150,000 price. I'll give you a $100,000 second mortgage for nine years at 7% annual interest and give you the $250,000 down payment."

While he is happy, you go on to explain the full details of your counter offer. "Here's how we'll handle the down payment. We will "split fund" the down payment as follows: At closing, I'll give you $150,000, and at the end of eighteen months I'll give you $100,000. Naturally, I will be making payments on the second mortgage each month in addition to this split funding of the down payment."

What you did, of course, was agree to the $250,000 down payment – only you won't pay it all at once. The net effect of this split fund is it will give you the opportunity to continue to raise the necessary funds from other investors during the eighteen months, or use funds you have from some other source.

Heck, if you wanted, since you bought such a good deal, you will increase the value of the property within the eighteen months and can get other financing or sell the property for a nice profit. You essentially controlled a larger asset with fewer dollars.

## A Six-step Checklist for Establishing a Group Investment Partnership

Follow this 6-step process to set-up your group investment partnership. This process covers critical functions a sponsor needs to complete to be successful.

**1. Prepare the Private Placement Memorandum (PPM):** In preparing this extensive document, the sponsor should engage the assistance of qualified legal counsel to make sure the document is properly put together. If you are syndicating your first group investment, then I highly recommend you obtain the guidance from local legal counsel.

**2. Prepare the Offering Circular:** To help expedite the marketing program, the sponsor should prepare a simple, one to four page brochure that includes the facts on the proposed offering.

**3. Obtain Securities Clearance:** Federal and state law clearance or registration must be complete before offering securities to investors. Each of the fifty states has different rules and regulation governing the sale of real estate securities.

Fortunately, many types of securities and many transactions in securities, are exempt from state securities registration requirements. For example, many states provide for transactional exemptions for Regulation D private offerings, provided there is full compliance with SEC Rules 501-503.

However, though certain types of offerings or transactions may not require registration, many states require filings or place additional conditions on exemptions available for many different offerings for which exemptions are available.

The best advice, then, is before offering any security for sale in any state, experienced counsel should be retained to review the applicable state laws and take any action necessary to permit the offering to be made in the particular state.

**4. Market the Offering to Potential Investors:** Now that your PPM is complete and is in compliance with state and federal security law regulations, you can market your investment opportunity to potential investors. Take the list of potential investors you have created and send your PPM to them. Since the PPM is confidential, make sure only the intended potential investor reads the contents. Finally, make a detailed record of all the potential investors that have received your PPM.

**5. Review the Investor Subscription Package:** As the LLC member interests are sold, each investor should send the copy of the subscription booklet and a check for the member interest purchased. The sponsor should carefully review the subscription booklet to make sure that all the requested information is completed and that the investor meets the suitability requirements of the transaction.

If any of the information is not correct, the sponsor should notify the investor to correct the information or notify the investor that they do not meet the suitability requirements. After careful review of this package, the sponsor should sign off on the various documents in this package.

**6. Set up an Escrow Account for the Initial Contributions:** Prior to any investor contributions being collected, the sponsor should set up an escrow account with a local bank. The bank should have a set of the instructions as to how and when to break escrow and to distribute these collected funds.

Another way to handle step 6 is to have each investor send money directly to the real estate escrow account. All of money from investors will be in the escrow account for closing of the investment property. Normally, from all the money sent to escrow from the investors, there will always be excess funds after closing. The escrow or title company will send the new buyer (investment group LLC) the balance of the funds. Take this check and deposit it into the new LLC partnership account. This partnership account will be used to operate the partnership until the property is eventually sold.

## Managing the Investment Group Partnership

Now that the deal is closed, the sponsor takes on the responsibility of managing the investment group partnership. These tips will help you be more successful with your investors and the investment asset.

As the sponsor, or managing partner, you will normally have 100% control of the operation of the investment group partnership. You are involved with the day-to-day operations of the property, whether you have hired a property management company or you are doing the management yourself. Ultimately, the responsibility for the success of the investment property remains with you.

As the managing partner of the investment group partnership, you will have far reaching and diverse responsibilities. You can commit contractual matters, order services, buy supplies, engage professionals, and bind the investment group partnership in any way deemed advisable to carry out the purposes of the investment group partnership business. Your investors are counting on you to deliver the results, outlined in the private placement memorandum.

### Hiring Professional Property Management Services

Since the investment group partnership will require active management, you will be tasked with hiring a good property management company to handle the day-to-day operations. Whether you will handle the property management duties or engage another professional property management company, you must have a management contract. The management contract should spell out the functions and responsibilities of the property manager in return for the fee to be paid. Typical management fees ranges from 5 to 10 percent of income collected on smaller properties and 3 to 5 percent of income collected on bigger properties.

## Investor Relations & Partnership Reporting

Contrary to on-going asset management duties for which fees are justified, fees are usually not justified by the sponsor for investor relations. Keeping investors informed of partnership asset performance is an expected sponsor duty and, in fact, is very important to the sponsor's current and future career goals. Although it is a simple and easily overlooked task, a regular brief quarterly status report does more good for an investor's sense of well-being than just about anything else a sponsor can do.

The most important point about investor relations is this: A very little amount of time and effort spent to keep your investors informed buys you a lot of mileage. Do not assume they know what's going on. Do not keep problems from them (except the minor day-to-day operating problems). Always be responsive if an investor asks for special information. These existing investors are your best source of investors for new deals. If they have been made to feel important and informed, they will go into your next deal with you as long as they have the money.

## VALUE INVESTOR PROFILE
*An Interview with Rory Maguire*

# *Creating Joint Ventures with Private Equity Capital*

Rory Maguire is President of Realty Capital Partners (RCP), a top private equity provider to smaller real estate sponsors. RCP is uniquely positioned to provide equity to sponsors that are just under the large institutions' radar screen of $10 million, with average equity investments of $1 to $5 million. Rory gives you a "behind the doors" look at how private equity providers partner with real estate sponsors. Learn the process from beginning to end on how to you can partner with companies like RCP.

**RCP's private equity investments are just under the radar screen of the large institutions. Tell us about RCP and its unique business platform.**

RCP is historically focused on what we would consider to be a small to mid-market property size. In general, we have invested in projects with total capital requirements from $10 million to $40 million. We feel that there is a lot of opportunity in that size range of deals. It is below the institutional radar, where they (investors) are looking these days to place as little as $10 million, but historically at least $20 million. It is a little larger deal than what a small real estate group might put together with their friends and family or for the so-called country club money.

And so within that range, there are a number of deals. They tend to be fairly straight-forward, easy to understand, require a relatively small investment, and we feel that there is a fair amount of opportunity there, just based on lack of competition from others.

**You began raising a new fund called the RCP Distressed Property & Income Fund. Tell us about this fund and how it will capitalize on the distressed commercial real estate market.**

We are working on a couple of funds right now. Ultimately, what we have been looking at and investing in over the last year and a half or so, are any numbers of asset types, with the common characteristic of income. We're looking for investments that can provide either current income, day one, or that we feel there is a pretty clear path to get to income within a relatively short period of time.

The fund, and the purpose behind that, is that we are seeing more and more opportunities requiring you to move very quickly. We've historically taken 60 to 90 days from start to finish to close a transaction, and today we are seeing a need to move a little faster than that. We are hoping these funds will allow us to do so.

**You recently invested about $2.5 million into two Dallas office buildings totaling roughly 170,000 square feet. Tell us about this deal and where you see the opportunity and value.**

We invested a little over $2.5 million in about 170,000 total square foot of office. One building, the smaller of the two, was 100% leased to a credit tenant, and the other being roughly 80% leased. GE Capital is our lender and our financial partner on the deal, and the total capital stack was probably in the neighborhood of $10.5-$11 million. From a valuation standpoint, we just love the deal. It's at kind of the intersection of Main and Main in Dallas, if you will, at Mockingbird and 75.

The deal came to us from the existing owners, which is a common theme among most investments we have made in the last 18 months. They are a local, regional office and mixed-use owner/sponsor. They have close to a billion square feet, so they are certainly not small. Historically, they have had all institutional relationships, including the equity investor in this project who invested roughly $10 million when they first purchased it.

That equity investor, like so many institutional partners we hear about today, has a fund that had wound down, and so they were looking to dispose of all assets in the fund. In many cases, the people are recalling their equity, and there are all kinds of issues. Here, the fund had wound down. This fund is a major fund and easily recognizable in New York that was no longer getting any fees, so let's dispose of all the assets at next to nothing. In this case, they took a backseat to all of our equity. Once we have made a two multiple on our investment, they receive a one-time check for $250,000.00. It is a pretty incredible opportunity.

I believe we're in the deal at roughly $65.00 a foot for great office space at a great intersection in Dallas, and going in, they won. We're hitting close to 12%. In fact, we just made a first distribution, and it was 12% return annualized for our investors. That is exactly what we are focused on doing today.

**When deciding to invest equity with a sponsor in a deal, what 4 or 5 criteria must the sponsor and the deal meet to attract your investment capital?**

First and foremost is track record and a good reputation in the market. We are looking for groups that understand a market like the back of their hand, and they will certainly have been there. They are not ones that are flying into a market, looking at a piece of property, and saying, "Oh, let's buy it". They are the guys that have lived there and been on the ground in that market for a long time. From there, any number of things could affect us.

As I mentioned earlier, debt can always play a major role. There could be any type of execution issues that we need to review. What it comes down to these days is sponsors are trying to be very optimistic with how they look at properties. Most packages we receive will have a lot of assumptions related to that optimism, the ability to grow the income stream, and we have got to be pretty conservative how we look at that. It's not an easy thing raising money these days, and certainly, you want to be arguing how conservative you are in your approach. It has caused us to turn down a lot of deals, but certainly, the good sponsors out there can find them.

**When you invest capital with a sponsor, how much do they need to put into the deal?**

It varies. I would say, in the last year, it's typically between 5 and 20%. An average for us is in that 5 to 10% range. There are other things that can go along with that. A personal guaranty on a loan, certainly, can speak to commitment. But we are looking for a co-investment, in general, of 5 to 10% to satisfy what we are looking for.

**What does the entire process look like from the time a sponsor brings you a deal through the time of closing?**

We are very typical of most equity investment groups. From the time a project comes in, our acquisitions team begins analyzing it as quickly as we can. We have done an analysis on it, both from what we call a back of the envelope analysis from a financial standpoint, or financial analysis standpoint. We also understand all the characteristics behind the project and what competitive advantages the sponsor believes it has.

Ultimately, if it has passed muster with our acquisitions group, it will go to our investment committee, which meets once a week, and we will review it as a company. Our committee is made up of 4 folks on the real estate side, and 4 on the capital market side. So you have a balance there of the people beating up the actual real estate deal, as well as people saying, "Is this the right deal for the market and how we are raising capital?"

From there, assuming the deal is approved, it goes through the typical letter of intent type process. Once that is complete, we go immediately into underwriting and preparing an investment package. The investment package, along with the partnership and the PPM are sent to our investor base. Currently, we have about 1,500 accredited investors. Not all of those are individuals. Some of those are financial planners with family office type groups.

The investment opportunity is literally packaged up and sent out. People can kick the tires on that one deal. We take commitments, collect capital and prepare for a funding as we are getting through all the legal documents with our sponsor.

That is a very typical process on a one-off deal. We do have funds that can look at certain other things, such as, distressed residential and some other aspects of real estate, but in general, that would be the process that a sponsor would go through with us.

**How long does it typically take to get feedback when a sponsor brings you a deal that has the deal tied up and they are under a time pressure?**

We pride ourselves on a quick response. I would say on the outside, it takes us two weeks, and most of the time, within a week. We also know when something isn't a fit right away and we don't need to spend too much time on it if we know it just doesn't work. If we think it might be, then we will get an answer out within a week or two.

**How does RCP typically structure equity JV deals with sponsors?**

We fall in line with the market as far as structure is concerned. We are going to underwrite to an income stream. So whether we are working with a sponsor who prefers an IRR waterfall or some type of structure with changing hurdles, or another sponsor who may just want to look at this as a straight split after a certain preferred return, either way would be very typical for us. Lot of deals these days kind of fall in a 10% preferred (return), 60/40 to 70/30 type range, 60 or 70% going to the equity, 30 to 40% going to the sponsor.

**A lot of sponsors generate fees through acquisition and other types of fees. How do you deal with that?**

In a very general sense, everyone is pretty shy of fees these days. Even in our business, it is very difficult to find investors if they feel like they are paying a lot of fees when they are giving you money to invest.

We are really seeing a big change in the fee structures and how those are put together these days. Everyone wants to see fees based on performance. You can get paid, but get paid after you perform for the investor. The sponsor fees are challenging. The development groups and sponsors out there are looking to find ways to keep the lights on right now. They are certainly hungry for those acquisition fees or ongoing management fees. We tend to put some performance measures in place.

It is a cool structure for us. There are 2 things. One, have they created a lot of value? Did they put it under contract and actually find a tenant to take half the building? Have they created significant value since they've gained control of the property but before they acquired it? In that case, then they have already performed, in our mind, in certain ways, and should be paid all or part of an acquisition fee.

In other circumstances, they have not performed yet, but do have a business plan in place; it's fairly easy to identify and execute; and we'll just tie fees and the release of those fees to the performance, based on the plan.

**The single family housing market has really taken a heavy hit. To capitalize on this opportunity, you have created a fund called, RCP Distressed Residential Property II Fund. Tell us about your plan to invest this capital.**

To date, we've invested starting end of November, beginning of December, 2009, about $10 million in distressed residential real estate. What we started with was, first of all, working with a group – a sponsor – that put together fairly sophisticated software and a great business model for how to acquire bulk residential real estate from lenders. It is a package of homes, and those homes are typically trading for far below market value because, as one can imagine, Bank of America has a real difficult time paying attention to a $125,000.00 house in North Atlanta. They don't have the ability to even focus on that small of a detail.

There are a lot of special servicers out there, waving their hands, saying, "We can handle it; we can handle it. We'll hire brokers, and you'll get maximum value." What a lot of those groups tend to be doing is pumping up the values a little bit so the Bank of America decision-maker is saying, "Oh, this looks pretty good, still." Nine months later, they've sold 1/3 of the homes and eaten up a ton of transaction costs with their servicer, realizing, "Wow, if we would have just dumped these things for 20% less, we could have been out of this thing on day one and had the cash to work with."

That tells you a little bit about the program that we have been investing in. It is the purchase of homes, somewhere between 50% and 60% of what we believe their value is today using fairly sophisticated models and certainly a local broker giving their broker opinion of value. It all goes into this matrix and this equation. A bid is put together, and we are purchasing packages from regional lenders, national lenders, certainly a bunch of banks you would recognize. When we do turnaround, we have a local broker that we've developed relations with through our sponsor company. They list the home and sell it. And it's a pretty impressive thing to see. It moves very quickly.

Our partner has in 2009, purchased roughly 420 homes. They averaged a little less than 90 days to sale. These are all equity models, and their target value, they hit right at 101% of what they felt they could sell these at, averaging about a one and a half multiple. If you can turn things and make a one and a half multiple in 90 to 120 days, you are doing pretty well. We are well-invested into that platform. Investors seem to love the all-equity nature of it, and that it turns pretty fast, so you don't feel like your capital is out there too long.

We actually bought a condominium in Las Vegas on Las Vegas Boulevard. We're thinking, "Oh, this is awful." And our sponsor said, "Trust us; this is what we do every day." And we did. A month and a half later, we bought a condo for $250,000.00, and sold it for $850,000.

It was the single best deal they had ever done in the history of their company, which we were happy to be a part of. It has been a pretty fun story to tell. It is a very interesting platform with the number of homes that we have seen this year, even the number of foreclosures are up over last. We do think this will be a viable platform for a few years.

**Rory Maguire**
President, Realty Capital Partners

Over the past 18 years, RCP has provided over $300 million of equity capital and secured loans to over 150 partnerships representing real estate assets throughout the United States in a broad array of sectors: retail, multi-family, hospitality, office, residential, industrial, mixed-use and land. Mr. Maguire is responsible for the operations of Realty Capital Partners, as well as analyzing and selecting real estate investment opportunities.

# Chapter 9

# Managing and Executing Your Value Investment Strategy

*"We can stabilize a property relatively very quickly. I like ones, like the one we just bought. It's 60% occupied with 288 units which gives me 100 units to immediately work on, and I have my own team for renovating those units. We can knock out 40 units a month, and so I can have those 100 units out real quick, and put those on the market at the same price as the guys across the street that have old, dated units. They get leased up immediately."*

Charlie Young
Madera Companies

You've spent the last number of months finding, negotiating, financing, and closing your new opportunity. Now it's time to create value on your new property using one or more of the value investment strategies discussed in this book. Your role and scope has transitioned from transactional to operational where executing the value creation strategy involves the basics of blocking and tackling. A lot of expertise and knowledge is involved in the operational side of the business so outsourcing these professional services is advisable, if you lack such expertise.

Experienced management and construction companies have a number of years under their belts executing within their expertise. They have time tested systems and a team of professionals to carry out the day-to-day property functions. The most important challenge you will have is finding and qualifying a great property management company and construction company.

Create a plan and focus your attention on coordinating and communicating your plan to your professional team. Provide the necessary oversight so that your plan stays on budget and on time. The two biggest challenges you will face executing your strategy will be controlling spending and managing the time schedule of the project completion.

## Creating Your Action Plan

Your action plan should contain five basic elements: a mission statement, objectives, strategies, tactical plan, and follow-up reviews. Having these basic elements in an action plan allows for a focused and targeted implementation of the plan.

1. **Mission Statement**: Identifies the purpose of the mission. This is the statement that best describes why your property will exist, its basic purpose and the end result of your value investment strategy.

2. **Objective**: Without an objective, the organization is like a ship without a rudder, going around in circles. It's like a prison escapee that has nowhere to go. Developing and communicating an objective, a unified sense of direction to which all members of the property can relate, is probably the most important concept in management for top-level consideration, and yet it is frequently overlooked. Unless the property, its people and management have an objective, properly identifying a philosophy of what they are in business for (and some plans to achieve these objectives), then there is not a unified direction that management can use to relate to day-to-day decisions.

   Objectives are general statements about what needs to be accomplished to meet the purpose, or mission, and address the major issues facing the property.

3. **Strategies**: The current methods of developing strategies have two fundamental problems that severely limit the likelihood of good decisions coming out of the process. The first problem is that strategic planning requires reasonably

accurate long-term forecasts, and yet such forecasts are almost always impossible to produce. The second problem is that most strategic plans are, in practice, not much more than financial hopes filled with "nice" numbers. Usually they are quantitative extrapolations of the past. Instead, they should center on pinpointing the strong and weak parts of the property and spelling out what actions are to be taken to eliminate weakness and to build on strength.

4. **Tactical Plans**: The fourth element in a strategic action plan is to figure out "How to get from here to there." This requires tactical plans. These plans are specific actions that are implemented to carry out a strategy.

    For example, if a strategy was developed to reposition an apartment property toward families, then some tactical plans might be to add a playground to the property, target the marketing toward this demographic, or create an after school program for the kids. Implementing these three tactical plans will carry out the strategy of repositioning the property toward families.

5. **Follow-up reviews**: A successful plan just doesn't happen; it must be continually followed and altered along the way making changes as the need arises. Any changes made are done to keep the plan in line with its objectives set forth in the fourth element.

Build your action plan around these 5 steps. As the property owner, you will ensure that the execution of your plan is being carried out by your team of professionals. Proper oversight is critical to the success of executing the plan.

**Managing the Progress of the Action Plan**

You can have a great plan and not succeed because of poor oversight of the action plan. You need to set up an effective management oversight system whereby you can coordinate the proper execution of the plan. There are four critical factors in managing the execution of the action plan.

1. **Communication**: All lead members of your team need to effectively communicate among themselves as a group. You will most likely have a management and construction leader. Both leaders need to be on the same page because many times there is overlap of responsibilities that requires good communication. I recommend weekly, in person or conference calls, with these key leaders to manage, review and forecast issues.

2. **Stay on Budget**: Staying on budget and managing costs is very important. Going over budget causes increased pressure on the success of the project.

3. **Plan Implementation**: Review the progress of your action plan regularly. Make sure all of your team leaders are staying on track with implementation of all the strategies in your plan. You developed a good plan so make sure everyone sticks to it.

4. **Measuring the Progress:** Keep tabs on how your plan is unfolding. Do you see improvements? What kind of feedback are you getting? Do you need to change anything to correct a problem? Be prepared to alter your plan if you see problems arising as you implement the action plan.

## Positioning Your Property

Positioning a property is a developed strategy to meet the market demands of a narrowly defined target market. Through your research from both the existing tenants and local market consumers, you were able to identify a group of people that have common characteristics. This group segment becomes your target market, the most likely candidate to rent at your property. By taking the characteristics of your property and matching them with the wants, needs and desires of your target market, you are positioning your property to gain a high percentage of rentals in this target market segment.

So, positioning is aligning your property's strengths with the likes, wants and needs of a small market segment. By positioning your property, you will be able to distinguish it among your competition and thus make it unique and different. By making it unique and different, you will be able to create a specific image for your property that allows you to stand out in the marketplace and thus allow your marketing efforts to be much more effective.

If part of your action plan is to reposition the property, then repositioning the property requires consistency among the various functions on the property. Marketing and management need to execute tactics that will produce the repositioning. Any new reconstruction that is done needs consistency with the likes, wants and desires of the target market. With a property being repositioned in the marketplace, the new property's business and physical environment must bring about the target market's feeling of comfort and fitting in with the property.

## Case Study

*I purchased a small 20-unit apartment building back in 1992 through a short sale with the lender and created value through revitalizing the property and positioning it toward a specific target market.*

> **Problem**: *The property was suffering with 30% vacancy, some deferred maintenance, and located in a declining neighborhood.*

> **Solution:** *An intense study was done to determine the resident profile to position the property. The property had a younger resident profile that was into punk rock, art, nature, and thought some of the deferred maintenance*

*added character to the property. An aggressive marketing campaign was created. It included an effective marketing message that was directed toward the resident profile target market. The marketing message was placed in medium where the target market would most likely see the message, such as music stores, art stores, coffee shops, and current residents.*

***Results:*** *New rentals came flooding into the small apartment building over the following two months. The property occupancy reached 100% with a waiting list as this property became the place to live for punk rock, art lovers. In short order, the property value doubled.*

## 4 Cornerstones to Successful Real Estate Investment Properties

Here are the four cornerstones that should be built into your real estate value investment strategy:

- Competent management
- Viable business plan
- Motivated team effort
- Financial resources

### Do You Have a Great Business Operator Running Your Property?

The number one reason a property struggles is from poor management. According to Herbert Woodward, "Business problems are due, not to bad luck, but to recurring patterns of non-constructive conduct by management."

An investment property is a business and has its own income statement, balance sheet, must operate within a budget, needs to remain competitive with other properties, has financing that needs servicing, and has a continuing need to keep its current customers, as well as, attract new ones. The better the property manager is at running your rental business, the stronger your investment will be.

## Do You Have a Viable Business Plan?

Having a viable business plan that tells a realistic story about the real estate investment business and how to best position the property greatly increases the likelihood of solid financial and operating performance. A viable business plan accomplishes the following:

- Provides a road map
- Helps determine a competitive business advantage
- Requires finding answers to tough questions
- Establishes a system of checks and balances

## Do You Have a Motivated Team Effort?

A motivated team can reach mountain tops with the right attitude. Most success can be traced back to attitude. Does your management team have the attitude and belief that they are going to be successful on achieving the goals in the business plan?

- Do team members look for ways to contribute to the project?
- Is your team excited about the success of the project?
- Does the team run the property like they own it?

## Do You Have the Financial Resources to Succeed?

Having adequate financial resources to run a real estate rental business is critical to a property's performance. A reality check for property owners and managers is that controllable and uncontrollable miscalculations and mistakes happen. So, planning for mishaps to occur in one's financial modeling is critical to achieving top performance. Create reasonable operating models that include adequate capital reserves. Finally, make certain the property has the financial wherewithal to access additional capital resources.

## Maximizing Financial and Operational Performance

Measure your rental property business using the four cornerstones to a successful real estate investment. Do you have solid management? Do you have a targeted business plan? Do you have good team motivation? Do you have the needed funds to effectively execute your targeted plan?

It is important to mention again that all four cornerstones must be successfully executed to create a solid foundation for optimum performance. A good plan executed with poor management can create underperformance. A good management team with a poor plan can also create underperformance.

So, if hiring a top notch property management company is critical to a property owner's success, what are the important ingredients to look for when you are in the process of hiring a property management company?

## Hire a Solid Property Management Company

Have you ever wondered why some properties seem to grow and prosper, even in tough economic times or in tough rental markets, while others struggle with sizeable negative cash flow?

Having worked with literally hundreds of struggling property owners and managers over the last 25 plus years, I have seen firsthand the many mistakes owners and managers make. And believe me, there are many types of mistakes. In fact, I've committed many of them at one time or another.

You know what I learned? I discovered the biggest mistake that 70% of all property owners were making, causing their properties to suffer, was BAD MANAGEMENT - costing them thousands upon thousands of dollars.

This mistake was being made by all types and sizes of property owners and all types and sizes of proprieties.

- It didn't matter whether you owned an 800 unit building or a 4 unit building

- It didn't matter if you were in the "business" full time

- It didn't matter if you had schooling and professional certifications or designations.

Property owners find many ways to get themselves into difficulty, but hiring bad property management ranks as the biggest mistake apartment owners make that drives their properties into the ground.

There are many management companies that represent themselves as reputable and experienced, but do not have a history or proven track record managing specific business plans or lifestyle properties.

Bad management is like having an inexperienced and unproven pilot flying a plane or captaining a ship that you are a passenger on. Bad management is like having an operation done by an inexperienced doctor. You might get lucky reaching your final destination or reaching your goal, but there is a much higher probability you will have serious problems along the way. I can safely say the number one reason properties fail is because of bad management as I outline in my book, "*How to Take an Apartment Building from Money Pit to Money Maker.*"

## Find the Best Property Management Company

Hiring a great property management company is your single most important thing to do as a property owner executing a value creation strategy. There are a lot of bad property management companies in the market so your job is to filter through the bad companies and find the best.

## Top 7 Considerations When Hiring a Property Management Company

There are 7 essential property management considerations to assess during your search for today's best management company. All property management companies are NOT created equal. Good management companies must:

1. Run your business like they own it
2. Hire the best people
3. Have a proven track record
4. Work well with you
5. Be connected with lots of resources
6. Know the market intimately
7. Know your product type

If you're a property owner, chances are you have several priorities. You want to make sure you're executing the value enhancement strategy, assets are well protected, your buildings are properly insured, maintained, and are secure. You want to maximize value, keep the space leased at market rates or above, and invest in needed improvements. And you want to control your costs— have tenants pay their fair share of operating expenses, manage vendor charges, and generally, maximize your investment.

Unless you are a professional property manager, this isn't easy. Property management is incredibly complex, detail-oriented, and time-consuming. And most likely, you have better things to do with your time like find great deals.

A good property management company will have a proactive approach to maintenance and market positioning, ensuring the value of your property is protected and enhanced over time. Management companies are experts at marketing, leasing, contract management, vendor management, accounting, and can assist with market research. Equally important, their systems for controlling costs and collecting for operating expenses can reduce lost revenue, which go right to your bottom-line.

# Renovating a Property

The goal of a renovation is to change the image of the property, as the marketplace perceives it, and improve the condition and functionality of the property.  Depending on the extent of the renovation and weather, it could take anywhere from two weeks to nine months to finish the project.

### Picking a Contractor

Most inexperienced business leaders usually pick the cheapest bid to do the work.  In fact, they will even brag about "the great deal they got."  The cheapest contractors tend to hire the cheapest laborers, which produce the poorest results in the longest time period.  Their motto is, "They don't have time to do it right the first time, but they have time to come back and do it again."  You simply get what you pay for, and in a renovation situation, time is extremely valuable.

A while back, I was consulting for a large owner on the west coast who was involved with a $1.2 million renovation to a property that was 36% occupied.  The owner took it upon himself to hire the general contractor to complete all the interior and exterior renovation work around the property.  This contractor was from out-of-state, but was very cheap.

The property did not have any apartment rent-ready units available to rent so it was basically out-of-business.  It took the contractor 2 ½ months before he delivered any rent-ready units to the owner.  The long delay on getting rent-ready units ended up costing the owner about $47,000 in lost rent and added costs.

When deciding on a contractor to hire, make sure you hire a company that charges a fair price and has a proven track record for getting the job done on time.  It's better to pay a few extra bucks up front and save on the backend.

### Where to Start the Construction?

The question always comes up, where is the best place to start the construction?  Because all renovations are unique, my standard answer is, it depends.  The most important thing to have is a space to rent so get something to lease first.

Just like washing your car, start from the top and work your way down.  Roofs are the very first thing to do with landscaping and parking lots toward the end of the renovation project.

You will get a lot of people nosing around your property when they see construction occurring on the property.  So to generate some excitement, start by making improvements on the front curb.  Continue to make improvements along the leasing path.  Now focus on improving the leasing office, making it look appealing and sexy.

Lastly, renovate a couple of vacant spaces so that you have something nice to show new prospects.  Ideally, begin the renovation with an improved front curb, leasing office and a few staged spaces to show.

## Managing the Construction

Make sure everyone is on the same page.  On the first day the construction company is scheduled to be at the property to begin work, set up a group meeting at the property with all the key people from both the property management and construction companies.  Create a game plan on the projects that get done first and the ones that will be done last.  Set up in advance a weekly progress meeting with the same key leaders.  Since good communication throughout the renovation will be important, make sure everyone understands this point.  If you accomplish all of these tasks in the first meeting, then you will have set a great foundation to begin your renovation.

Managing the construction requires inspection of the work while it is in progress, as well as, after it has been completed.  Inspections are important to follow the progress, find problems, and to communicate your findings to your partners.  Also, inspections are done to make sure the contractor is complying with the construction agreement and staying on schedule.

The inspection punch sheet is a tool that is used to sign off on construction work as it pertains to the scope of work outlined in construction agreement. Once you sign off on the work, the construction company is no longer responsible for anything that happens. So, make sure everything that was supposed to be done, is correctly done.

# How to Renovate and Reposition Value Add Multifamily Properties

Charles Young is Co-founder and Principal of Madera Equity, headquartered in Lubbock, Texas. Madera Equity is a small multifamily syndication boutique firm that has successfully capitalized on renovating distressed properties since 1991. Charlie uses a simple, "cookie cutter" value add business plan that involves buying 1980's properties, spending $10,000/unit on renovations, repositioning the property to a stronger demographic group, and raising rents about $150/unit per month.

Find out from Charlie why their strategy of being good and not being big has helped his company deliver a strong performance for almost 20 years. Charlie is executing value creation strategy No. 2: Buying lower class properties and repositioning them to high class properties.

**Can you tell us a little bit about Madera?**

All we've done from day one is multifamily. That's it. I bought my first apartment deal at the end of the RTC days, in 1990. All of our deals have been value-add deals. We take C properties and completely renovate them, typically on average about a $10,000 a unit rehab. Putting them back together, turning them from C's to B's, and going from there.

**Would you say there's anything unique or different about your model?**

We are a vertically integrated company, so there's nothing that we outsource. I am the partner who's responsible for markets, acquisitions, and most of the equity. I've got a partner who is totally responsible for operations, a partner totally responsible for rehab transitions, and another partner that we're firing up a fund right now, and we brought another partner in that has experience in funds and that side of the business, and so we're very hands-on. We don't do a lot of projects. I'm not looking for volume; I'm looking for good deals that we can do two to three, maybe maximum of four a year, and very hands-on. We've got a very senior team. Most of our people have been with us for a long time - some of them 15 years. And so we've got a very experienced group that knows 1980s and 1990s vintage apartments and what it takes to put them back together, and that's what we do.

## What do you consider a good value add deal?

Well, I'll give you two examples. We just closed a deal last week that was a 1984 vintage. It was a short sale with the lender. The previous owner had owned it since 2001, right at $14 million of debt on 288 units. We got it for $6 million, right at 45 cents on the dollar. That sounds great, but you've got to take the sub-market and say, "We want our deal to be the lowest basis with the best quality in that particular sub-market." It gives us a competitive advantage. Texas is our market that we play in predominately because in Texas, the markets do this dramatically. We have gone to Florida, Indiana, Arizona, but have consolidated back to Texas.

Houston and Dallas are our primary markets. And so if you buy what's considered stabilized, cash on cash deal, and the market goes against you, you're either breaking even or you're broke. You could take a value-add deal, and create value out of it, and put margin in it, and you're good to go if you don't get out on time. We used to do some deals in College Station. Had a great value-add deal in a market that we bought in 2001 and sold in 2004. This was before the student housing guys came to College Station. Huge upside on the value-add side of this deal: 250 units. Had some partners, or some friends that wanted a cash on cash deal. At the time, College Station was 96% occupied, no student housing. Everybody thought it was great, so two buildings down, we bought 144 units, and everybody thought they were going to get a 12% cash on cash. So the student housing guys come to town, and the market goes from 96 down to the 80s, and the cash on cash deal – we got out of it, broke even because we had some management upside on it, but still, the value-add deal we had – was one of the best deals we've ever done in a depressed market, so that was kind of my learning a lesson.

And so, I don't care what it is, where it is – I won't do something now that I cannot do a significant value-add play to it with the thought that okay, some of them I'm going to get out on top, and then there's some that the market will go against us at some point, and we will have created enough margin that we'll be able to still do well on it.

**You're looking for value-add. What strategies do you like the best?**

The key for us, right now, is updating the units all the way. So we take them, put all new flooring, all new fixtures, rework the cabinets, new counters, new appliances, and so that 1980s product is completely renovated. We try to get product that doesn't have a galley kitchen, that the majority of the units have washer-dryer connections, no boilers, no flat roofs. It's got to be a good mid-'80s product to '90s, where we can go in and do a like-new rehab on it.

**What about unit types?**

Well, that depends on the sub-market. I'm working on a deal right now in north Dallas that the whole sub-market has a preponderance of one-bedrooms, 75% one-bedrooms, and that's okay for that sub-market. So it really depends on that particular sub-market and what is in there. If you have a sub-market that has a huge mix of even product, and you buy a product that's 80% one-bedrooms, that may be problematic, and I wouldn't do that. There's one that we just closed for $20,000 a unit, in essence. The one I'm looking at now, in north Dallas, is going to be $30,000 a unit, at 1986 vintage. But the stabilized products that have been sold right around there have sold for $53,000 a unit, $50,000 a unit, $40,000 a unit, with a $12,000 rehab on it. So if I buy it for $30,000 a unit and put $10,000 into it, and I may do it for 40, my basis is still lower than my competition. That's what I look for.

**Are you rehabbing all the units?**

All of them, 100%

**When spending $10,000 per unit on interior rehab, what types of rent increases are you getting?**

$150 per unit per month

**How long does it take you to renovate a property, to get it stabilized?**

We can stabilize a property relatively very quickly. I like ones, like the one we just bought. It's 60% occupied with 288 units which gives me 100 units to immediately work on, and I have my own team for renovating those units. We can knock out 40 units a month, and so I can knock those 100 units out real quick, and put those on the market the same price as the guys across the street that have old, dated units, and they get leased up immediately.

I would prefer to have something 60-70% that's not that far off of what I would call just break even, and then move very quick – our competitive advantage is doing the rehab. I can do the rehab extremely quickly, faster and cheaper than most anybody else can, particularly on the interior units, turn them, and get them leased real quickly.

We can do the exterior in three months. The exterior and amenities, and the units, it takes a full 12 months.

**You rehab the units upon acquisition. You start a lease-up process to lease those rehabbed units out. When you lease all**

**the rehabbed units, do you wait until occupied units roll over?**

As those residents' leases come up, we give them the opportunity to take one of the newer units at the newer unit price, which very rarely they do, and they move on.

**Is there a Madera way that you renovate the exterior of your properties?**

Anything that is an eyesore to the outside. We always change the front – and the one that we're doing now is going to have kind of a southwest theme to it, with some gables and stone on it. And then go in and gut the whole office. The only thing left, probably, is the roof. And go back and recreate the space and what would be the best use of that space, whether it's a business center or a community center or whatever. You know, that's the disadvantage that we have, as you come with a limited amount of space and say you can only put, probably, one, maybe two good amenities, not the whole A product list, and so we try to figure out what is that one or two – What's going to give that bang when they walk in and go, "Wow."

**Is there something typical that you add?**

A community center that's got a game room, with a sports bar look, gets a huge amount of use, along with a coffee Internet café.

We'll have one room with a really nice coffee machine in it, and a couple of couches and a table, and it kind of goes between a business center and a café, and that gets used a good deal. Then out next to the pool, we'll put $30,000 into an outdoor kitchen cabana type of setting. They all will have their friends over on a day during the summer and sit out there, and it's just like them having a custom home with a nice pool and a nice amenity.

**At 10,000 a unit, you're doing a pretty good renovation. Do you change the name of the property?**

Yes, always.

**Can you come up with maybe three or four ideas – keys to your success – why you've been successful? What are you doing that's simple, that gets done right, that helps your success?**

We've been in the markets that we're in since 1995. Know your market, know your product. I can underwrite in Dallas and Houston quicker than anybody else. Number two is going to be the reposition strategy, and what we put on that, and we've done enough of them that we know what it takes. We go out and we shop our comps, and at the end of the day, we're going to end up with a higher quality product at a lower basis than anybody else. Our first and foremost strength was our management from our original days, and we have a very strong base in that area, and so we don't third party it out; we do it ourselves, and so the management expertise. Those are probably the four keys: buying it right, knowing it, rehabbing it, and running it.

**It's interesting you say the market. There are a lot of investors that want to go to different markets and buy properties. They don't realize that it's real important to understand the jungle you're going into and understand the market.**

You can take Houston, Texas, for example. It has 26 different – technically 26 different sub-markets. It just depends on which version you're looking at – whose data you're looking at. In Houston, Texas, you have to know where you can be and whether you can create value or not. I mean, that's the deal. I can go put $10,000 a unit into it, but if it's in a war zone, it's in an area that can't get my rent increases.

**Charlie Young**
Co-Founder, Madera Companies

Madera Equity is a real estate investment and management company solely focused on creating value in multifamily properties, through the acquisition and repositioning of distressed apartment assets that has completed over $100 million of acquisitions and dispositions. The Madera strategy has been to identify and acquire underperforming multifamily assets which suffer from operational ineffectiveness, deteriorating physical makeup or a combination of both.

# Chapter **10**

## *Winning the Game of Real Estate Value Investing*

*"I think anyone who does it right realizes that real estate is a get-rich-slow business, not a get-rich-fast business, and safety is the most important thing, and being fair to all involved."*

William "Rance" King, Jr
RK Properties

Look around and what do you see? Real estate is being offered at huge discounts to intrinsic values. It's time for you to get in the game and cash in on today's once in a lifetime buying opportunity. We are at a point in the real estate cycle where market timing couldn't be better. Because the current real estate down cycle was so deep and lasted so long, the next real estate boom cycle should be a long and steady ride. Real estate investors who catch this next wave will build long term wealth and find financial independence.

In 1991, I participated in the last big boom real estate cycle by buying and syndicating apartment buildings. We negotiated low prices, created value using the strategies mentioned in this book, made good cash flow and rode the appreciation wave during the boom cycle. In the late 90's, we sold our properties, where my investors and I made, on average, six times our initial investment.

I wasn't the only one that made substantial profits during the last real estate boom cycle. Many smart investors saw the same opportunity. In fact, if you look at some of the most successful real estate investment companies, you will find most of them started in the early 1990's, right at the boom of the cycle.

Many of the Value Investor Profiles outlined in this book are people who started back in the early 90's. If they did it, you can too.

It's my strong belief that in the next twenty years, one will look back at successful real estate investors and find most of them started in the 2010 to 2012 time period. This is your time. Don't miss this opportunity to be one of those successful companies that started during this market bottom.

The common reason I see for not taking action is due to fear. What do you have to fear? Making mistakes is part of life. Heck, I made a ton of mistakes back in the 1990's and still made a lot of money. The good thing about buying with good market timing is that the market boom cycle can save you. If I wouldn't have made so many mistakes back then, I could have made eight or nine times my money instead of only six times. The strong real estate market helped me work through my problems. If you learn this business from professionals using a simple system, supported by value real estate investing principles, you will be leaps and bounds ahead of most other investors.

It's not unusual to hear investors say, "I won't be able to find money partners to fund my deals." This is a big fear for new investors because they don't understand the inside game of value real estate investing.

I have met many group partnership sponsors and syndicators. Most tell me that in the beginning days they too were often "scared" or, at the very least, apprehensive. You might be surprised to learn that some of the largest investors in the world started with less than $10,000 on their first investment. Most new business undertakings take guts! But they made it – they proudly put together their first investment and now many are controlling multi-millions in property within two to three years. The "getting started" is the tough part. But with the right training, system, attitude, hard work, and support – you can do it too!

## Sample First Deal

Let's say, you find a small apartment property you can buy for $230,000, which previously sold for $500,000 a few years back. There is existing financing of $200,000, which can be worked out with the lender so that you can take over the loan. The only money you need to come up with is $30,000 for the down payment and an additional $30,000 for renovations, reserves, your fees, and closing costs, making the total capital to raise $60,000.

You do some research and find that through some minor property improvements and adding new management, the property will be worth $425,000 within 12 months after executing your value creation strategy. During your research, you find similar property sales of $300,000, if you sold the property without doing anything to the property, creating a nice cushion.

You create an investor package, which includes an overview on the property, a detailed business plan on your value creation strategy, supporting sales comps, and financial projections. You take this package to family and friends and show them the opportunity. Because you practice the principles of value real estate investing, your potential investors notice, in the investor package, that you have built in a margin of safety by buying the property for $230,000 when it's really worth $300,000. They also notice the thorough research you have done and that the investment looks to have a very attractive return. Because you have brought potential investors a great deal, they are motivated to invest in your deal. The biggest problem you will have is potential investors fighting over being left out on this deal because you are going to more than double their investment within a year.

Yes, you CAN find investors to fund your deals. Find a great deal that already has profit potential built into it. Also, start small by buying a property that doesn't require too much money to raise. Make sure you keep your first deal small and manageable. Getting a 'W' (win) is more important than hitting a home run. The deal size can get bigger as you buy more deals. Your existing investors will want to see your next deal, and they will refer other investors, creating a scenario where you will have more funds to buy a bigger deal.  Get the first one done and watch your funding raising efforts take off.

## Achieving Financial Independence with Group Investments

Unleash the Value Hound system of finding great deals that offer value creation opportunities and then syndicate them through group investments to create financial freedom for you and your family.  The process of finding great value real estate investments and finding investors for those real estate investments can become a business.  It's a real business that provides an income stream, by way of various syndicator fees, and builds long term wealth from backend performance profits. This business is often referred to as the syndication business.  By using a very conservative syndication model (shown later in this chapter), you can become a syndicator or sponsor full time in as little as three years and achieve financial independence.

The syndication model is a common model used in the purchase and sale of many types of assets, but for our purposes, it is used quite often with real estate investments.  Some of the largest investors in the country syndicate their properties.  In fact, every one of the Value Investor Profiles you've read about in this book syndicates their real estate investments.  I would venture to say that less that 10% of all large commercial real estate investments around the world are 100% owned by an individual or family unit.  Most large commercial properties are purchased by pooling investors together.  If you want to build financial independence through commercial real estate investment, then learning how to use the syndication model will help grow your real estate business.

Take for example William "Rance" King, Jr.  He graduated from college and worked as a business machine salesman for years.  In 1976, he syndicated his first small value add apartment building in California.  Rance's first investors were his co-workers at his place of employment.  Finding success with his first investment, Rance found a great value creation deal on another smaller apartment building, and again pooled investors together using the syndication model. Rance has been using the same syndication model for over thirty five years and has had over 126 properties go full cycle, where he bought and sold his properties, returning consistent cash flow and profits to his investors. During his thirty five years in business, he has made himself and his investors a lot of money. Today, Rance's real estate syndication business has grown to over $300 million.

Rance's syndication business consists of many activities in real estate investment, management and construction. Rance is actively involved with the acquisition of new properties, financing the properties, packaging and underwriting new investments for investors, managing properties and investors, construction related activities to build and renovate properties, and eventually selling properties for profits. All of these services take time and require expertise so Rance charges fees for the services he offers. These fees help pay for his support staff so that he can run his business and provide a comfortable life style for his family.

As Rance says, "This is a get rich slow business." Find a great value creation opportunity and raise the capital to fund the deal. Research and locate another great value creation deal and then raise the capital to fund the deal. Repeat the process over and over again, while building your long term wealth in the process.

## The Value Hound Blueprint to Financial Independence

I have created a very simple syndication model plan for you to follow. This model was created with a new investor in mind. Experienced investors can simply multiply the results by "X" number of times based on their experience level.

The purpose of this model is to give you a big picture of the potential of a value real estate syndication business. The blueprint must be modified to conform to your real world market conditions, but it gives you a starting point. This blueprint model offers you a "first draft" to tear apart and reassemble into your own particular plan. Have some fun and make you own assumptions and recreate your ideal model plan.

*Assumptions*

There are many ways to structure a partnership with investors. You may have a fantastic deal that has a lot of built in equity where you might want to take less fees and more backend profit. You might have a deal that has a lot of construction where you get paid construction fees to oversee the construction process. Some investors don't take any fees on their first deal and only participate in the backend. To keep it simple, I have created assumptions based on what might be in an average syndication model. Again, there is no hard and fast rule on how to structure your partnership but here are the assumptions for our model syndication plan:

- Acquisition fee of 3% of the purchase price.
- Underwriting fee 5% of the money raised for packaging and finding investors.
- Annual partnership fee 1% of the asset value.
- Resale fee of 3% of the sales price
- Sell a property every four years
- Sponsor (you) get 25% of profits
- Buying with a safety of margin

There are some fees you might want to add and others you might want to delete. For example, on a property I syndicated where we did a complete renovation spending almost $2 million, I took a construction fee of 5% of the construction budget to compensate me for services rendered in managing the construction process. Keep in mind the type of services you may render on your particular deal and add those fees into your model.

Some sponsors will find a property that requires extra capital for renovations that is not used in our sample model plan. Again, that's okay because your model plan can be a little different.

*Year 1*

Since you are new to the business and still learning the business, I have assumed you are going to buy one property for $300,000 and raise $100,000 from friends and family investors. We are buying commercial properties, but buying a house on your first deal is okay; I did. Also, remember that we are buying property with a margin of safety, which should be purchased significantly below market value. Your first deal has to be a "no brainer" for an investor. It should have a WOW factor that when potential investors look at your deal they get excited about the profit potential.

You have plenty of time to find a great value deal. When you contract to purchase the property, give yourself plenty of time to find investors, so ask for a 90-day close with two 30-day extensions when negotiating the purchase of the property with the seller. Don't agree to a short time fuse on your closing.

Normally, I prefer smaller investment groups. They are easier to manage. But in our sample model, as a new investor, you are trying to build a growing pool of investors so bigger is better on the first deal. While you might find one person to give you $100k, I want you to find ten investors with $10,000 each, which will raise a $100,000 for your first deal. Make sure you follow state and federal guidelines when raising money as mentioned in a previous chapter.

With the funds you have raised, you will make the planned down payment, pay closing costs, pay your fees, and have money left for reserves. The hardest part of the business, getting started, is now over. Your syndication business is now under way.

*Year 2*

As a result of having your first deal done, you are now viewed differently by potential investors. You are a deal maker and raising money starts to become easier.

In year 2, you are going to buy two properties that equal $700,000 in purchase price and raise $300,000 of equity from investors. Every six months you are going to find an awesome value deal and raise $150,000. I want you to raise $15,000 from 10 investors on the two investments. If possible, try to get as many new investors as possible. Ideally, by the end of year 2, you might have 30 different investors. This is a great size of investors to manage. In many cases, just making money for this pool of investors can be the very nucleus to raising additional money on future deals. Raising money can be as simple as going to your current investor base and having them invest and bring in other qualified investors.

*Year 3*

After two years of building your syndication foundation, you are ready to buy a bigger deal. I want you to buy a property for $1,500,000 and raise $600,000 of equity capital. You have a pool of investors to start fund raising, and because you've been doing this for two years, other investors have approached you looking to invest. If you followed our get-rich-slowly process, the third year will really be a big stepping stone for your business. It's quite possible you could buy a larger property, raising more than $600,000 because you have built a strong investor following.

You are making nice fees from your syndication business. With a six figure income, you can think about quitting your regular job and run your syndication business full time. You have found financial freedom in year 3, giving you lots of options.

*Year 4*

You will notice the syndication process flip flopping from when you first began. It's now easier to raise money than it is to find great deals. In year 4, be careful. This is where a lot of syndicators make a big mistake. You have a large investor pool of investors to fund deals. Many syndicators get greedy to earn fees and start buying properties that are more risky and don't offer a margin of safety. Follow the plan and only buy great value deals; you're a value investor. If it turns out you can place more money on great deals, then fantastic. But only buy great deals. It will pay off handsomely in the future.

Continue to buy larger properties because they offer better economies of scale. In year 4, you will buy a $2,000,000 property, raising $800,000. With all the investors chasing you to invest their money, make sure you buy a great value opportunity.

You will sell your first property in year 4. This will return money to your investors and make you a nice profit. Many times, investors will want to reinvest their sale proceeds into another deal so you'll have some available capital for another deal. I recommend you participate as an investor with your own money in the next deal. Your invested money will be treated the same as other investors, and you might negotiate a higher backend profit split because your money is in the deal. For purposes of our sample model plan, I have not assumed you will invest your money in the next deal.

*Year 5*

Things are really rolling now with your syndication business. You have become a real professional at buying undervalued real estate to profit for your investors. Your business has become quite busy so it's now time to hire support staff to help further grow your business.

Again, you will sell another property and distribute profits to your investors and yourself.

The last year, in our sample model plan, you are going to buy a $2.5 million property, raising $1,000,000. As the years roll by and your investor pool is large, you can now shorten your closing time frame. There may be some excellent buying opportunities that require you to move quickly so you now have the flexibility to do so.

*Year 6 and Beyond*

You have created sizeable wealth during the last five years. You only bought great deals using the real estate value investing principles mentioned in this book and got rich slowly. You weren't influenced by getting too big, too fast. Your investors are your biggest fans and they look to you with confidence to manage their money.

You have many options to continue your business. You can start buying value deals using most or all of your own money, giving you control and more profit potential. You can continue to grow your business by syndicating more deals. Your options are endless because you now have the American dream - financial independence.

## Sample Syndication Model Investment Plan

| | Initial | | | | Annual | | | | RESALE Sponsor | |
|---|---|---|---|---|---|---|---|---|---|---|
| | Raised | Purchase | Acquisition | Underwritting | Partnerhsip | | Sell | Resale | Profit | Income |
| Year | Capital | Property | Fee 3% | Fee 5% | Fee 1% | Sell | Property | Fee 3% | 25% | Total Per Year |
| 1 | $ 100,000 | $ 300,000 | $ 9,000 | $ 5,000 | $ 3,000 | | | | | $ 17,000 |
| 2 | $ 300,000 | $ 700,000 | $ 21,000 | $ 15,000 | $ 7,000 | | | | | $ 46,000 |
| 3 | $ 600,000 | $1,500,000 | $ 45,000 | $ 30,000 | $ 15,000 | | | | | $ 100,000 |
| 4 | $ 800,000 | $2,000,000 | $ 60,000 | $ 40,000 | $ 20,000 | 1 | $ 500,000 | $ 15,000 | $ 50,000 | $ 210,000 |
| 5 | $1,000,000 | $2,500,000 | $ 75,000 | $ 50,000 | $ 25,000 | 2 | $1,000,000 | $ 30,000 | $ 75,000 | $ 297,000 |
| 6 | | | | | | 3 | $2,100,000 | $ 63,000 | $150,000 | $ 273,000 |
| 7 | | | | | | 4 | $2,800,000 | $ 84,000 | $200,000 | $ 329,000 |
| 8 | | | | | | 5 | $3,500,000 | $105,000 | $250,000 | $ 380,000 |
| TOTAL SOURCE OF INCOME | | | | | | | | | | $1,652,000 |

Shown in the chart above, the left side of the plan is the acquisition or buy portion, and the right side of the plan is the disposition or sell portion. Properties are purchased each year for five years, and sold four years following the year of purchase. The annual partnership fee is not a onetime fee, like the other fees in the chart, so it is earned each year and is calculated in the total income per year.

This chart can be recreated using spreadsheet software like Excel. Build your own model. You might want to take less fees and more backend profit participation. You might want to take more fees and less backend. I know a syndicator that only took 10% of the backend but took much higher front end fees. You might want to invest a large portion of your own money and therefore require a higher backend percentage. You might be able to raise much more money than outlined in the sample plan. Create your own plan and take action on executing it.

Finally, solid real estate investments require cash down payments. The "no down" seminar hucksters are doing students an injustice by selling high risk opportunities. Most well thought out business plans require a capital investment to achieve a successful end result. Heavy debt loads financed with "no down" deals put a tremendous amount of stress on a property's ability to performed as planned. In fact, most lenders require a certain amount of equity capital. The group investment model, we have mentioned in this book, allows for investors to provide the sufficient capital required of best practice principles that increases the safety of an investment by its investors. If you have little to no money, then use the group investment model by using your efforts and hard work to uncover a great deal that investors find comfortable capitalizing.

## Taking Action

You're reading this book, which is a first step to taking action on your dreams. There is an unprecedented opportunity in the real estate market to make a lot of money for you and potential investors. Don't miss the opportunity. It's staring you right in the face. This is a simple business if you take it slowly and surround yourself with top notch experts.

Here's the very first thing I want you to do. Pick up the newspaper or search on-line for real estate property for sale. Look for opportunities. Get in your car and go look at the deals you find. Drive around and look at other properties. Look to see possibilities where you can create value. I want you to spend at least 3 hours during this entire process. Can you see the potential? Do you see opportunities?

Next, I want you to assess your emotions when you finish looking at properties. Are you excited? Do you feel hungry to be in the real estate game? If not, then not taking action might be the best alternative. Don't engage in any activity if there's no passion. You need passion to succeed.

If you do feel excitement and passion, then you'll be doing yourself a huge disservice if you fail to take action. Don't lose the passion. Keep looking for value opportunities. You'll be amazed at the actions you will take once you come across a great deal. Wow, you get hungry to get the deal done. You see no obstacles because deep inside, you know that if there's a will, there's a way to get something done, if you want it bad enough. If this is something you want bad enough, then I will be more than happy to point you in the right direction to get you started.

## How Long Do You Keep Doing Something That's Not Working?

How long do you keep doing something that isn't working, whether it has to do with your health, your business, your family, your investments, your future or whatever?

Just ask all the stock market investors a few years back who got demolished because they ignored reality. Gosh, I remember visiting a property and meeting a leasing agent that was a senior citizen. He was working part-time to earn some extra money to cover the shortfall on his retirement funds from his big losses in the stock market.

Do you recall when Enron's stock was at $90? Then it dropped to 80, then 70, then 60, 50, 40, and 30. Investors still stayed with the stock.

Then it went to 20, 10, 5, 3, and one measly dollar a share. They stayed with the stock.

Then it dropped to 90 cents, and to 80 cents. They still stayed with the stock. They whined about how they lost their money. I don't get it. When something isn't working, it's time to try something else.

Lots of people moan about how they aren't successful or how they aren't where they want to be in life. But when you examine what they're doing, you see the same thing over and over. You see someone who's afraid to make a change.

Don't be that person who is afraid of making change. You bought this book for a reason and that was to make a change. There are many successful people that will help you along your journey; all you have to do is ask for help.

One of my favorite quotes is from Lee Riley, father of the famous NBA basketball coach Pat Riley. He said, "Every now and then, somewhere, some place, sometime, you are going to have to plant your feet, stand firm, and make a point about who you are and what you believe in."

How about you? Are you ready to plant your feet and make a stand? Are you ready to make a change?

# How to Build a Successful Group Investment Company Buying Value Add Properties

William "Rance" King, Jr., Founder and CEO of R.K. Properties, headquartered in Long Beach, California, offers us a true real estate success story. Rance started buying small apartment buildings in 1976 using real estate syndications to buy distressed value add properties. After almost 35 years of doing the same things over and over again, Rance has built a $300 million+ family real estate business with over 126 properties going full cycle and generating safe and consistent cash flow for his investors.

Rance says the real estate business is a get rich "slow" investment, where safety and conservative investments over time creates real wealth. Rance came from an entirely different industry to start his real estate business so he didn't have any real mentors. He learned the real estate investment and management business the good ole fashion way, from the "school of hard knocks."

**You are the true value investor in the real estate business. Can you tell us a little about what your company does?**

We own and operate apartment buildings in six states and started in 1976 in California. About ten years ago we started going out of state. We like to add value, buy apartment buildings, and find a way to make them better.

## How did you get started in this business?

I've only done two things in my life: this, for 34 years, and business machines, for 10 years. I started as a salesman here in Long Beach for Victor Business Machines, which at the time, was a Fortune 500 company. I became top salesman in the country in pretty short order, and after about 3 years, they moved me to Seattle as a sales manager, and then San Francisco as a branch manager, and finally, back here as regional manager where I bought my first apartment building in San Francisco in the mid-'70s. Back then, Victor was just entering what would be kind of the equivalent of the PC business. Computers were very primitive back then, and we were trying to develop software because canned software like you find today didn't exist back then. So I said, "Well, let's develop some stuff for commercial real estate brokers." So I got to understand how the numbers work. My sales force was selling these machines and I bought my first apartment building. Then they moved me from the Bay area to here (Long Beach); then wanted to make me national director of sales and move me to Chicago. I was kind of their "boy wonder" back then. And I didn't want to go to Chicago, so I quit and started my company.

I started with a four-plex, a six, an eight, and sixteen, and grew up, and one of the reasons I left Long Beach was because, predominately, all that's here is older properties, and you have an awful lot of older properties with no onsite parking or very little onsite parking. So it was a big deal for me. I remember the year. It was the same year I built this building in 1984(referring to his original office). I went to Orange County and started buying. Just going over the river was a big jump. And then the Inland Empire, and then San Diego, and then out of state – probably the first property was in Las Vegas about 8 years ago.

## You syndicate and raise money from investors to buy your properties.

Well, in the beginning, it was all my friends from Victor Business Machines. I had already bought a few buildings and they said,

"Geez, next time you do one, I'd like to get involved". So I would do a deal where the three of us would each put in a third of the money. We'd buy a building and I would do the work so I'd take an extra 10% of the profits. Basically, I followed that same structure for years.

Once we became more involved with the broker-dealer community, and we structured our projects for the broker-dealer community, we had to go with more of a traditional kind of back-end than that.

**Did you ever get to the point that you maybe thought, "Gosh, this is kind of tough" and think about quitting?"**

I think the economy almost did that to me a few times. In 1981, I had bought 18 buildings. They were all little, but 18 buildings. You know, probably 6 to 20 units each. Interest rates, as you may remember, went through the roof. I think the prime hit 24% and mortgage rates were 18%. I can remember having money in a Merrill Lynch money market, getting 16%. People that didn't live through that can't even imagine.

It was amazing. And that's, of course, what brought about variable interest rate loans and everything else, but yeah, that was a very difficult time because by 1983 I thought, "Oh, my gosh, these buildings I bought in 1981 – I'm never going to be able to sell them at a profit." And of course, by maybe 1986, I did.

**So you're out there; you're starting a syndication business; you're new to the business, learning along the way like we all do. What are a couple of blunders that you had that you learned from?**

Probably – not a whole lot. I did one on a personal level, as I wanted to buy a home on the water in 1981, and so I refinanced a building that I owned to help give me the capital to buy that, and of course, that was a horrible time to do it, and I probably shouldn't have done that. But I survived it. And then, another interesting blunder – two, actually – would have been in the early '90s, during the next recession. You know, as you recall,

California was brought to its knees by what I call the "financial perfect storm" with change of the tax law in 1987, the over-building, the end of the Cold War, which devastated the defense industry, and I had sold a couple of buildings in 1985 or 1987, and one was to a doctor, and he put down, I think, a half a million dollars, and a million and a half dollar sale. Anyhow, I carried back a small note behind both of these two sales. When these guys went into default in the early 1990s and were basically losing the buildings to the bank, I stepped in and cured the debt and foreclosed, and there was really no equity to protect, and it was a dumb thing to do at the time because I used my cash when, on a go-forward basis, I could have used that cash. But those were really about the only two. And I still have one of those buildings today.

### How about a couple of big successes you had?

I would say that nothing really comes to mind because I make my deals pretty safe and I think I've had 126 buildings go full cycle, which in my business, you just aren't going to find anyone with that kind of track record.

Probably the biggest return I've ever had was maybe the first one I bought and I didn't know what I was doing. It was in the middle '70s and we'd just come out of a recession. It was just a little four-plex, and I bought it with 10% down. I think I made a 500% return on my investment in nine months but it was small numbers.

### You're going along and at some point – there had to have been a point where you said, "Okay, this is really starting to work." When do you think that was?

I think it's the cycles. I mean, the cycles feel good. 1976 through 1980 when my first cycle was great; 1986 through 1990 was great; 1990 through 1995 was a nightmare, but I started buying foreclosures in 1993, and bought nothing but foreclosures from 1993 to 1998. And then, of course, the current cycle probably ended two years ago, and now we're in a down cycle, but I can already start to see things starting to improve. I can see occupancy going up, and there aren't as many distressed sales out there with the kind of product that we deal with, as you might think.

**Rance, you're active in buying and selling properties, you're active with property management business, you're active in the brokerage business, you're active in placing debt and equity, construction – what do you enjoy the most?**

Doing deals. I like acquisitions. I love buying the property. Selling the property, in a normal market, you know, today everything is the Internet. You put it out there, where it used to be maybe the *L.A. Times* or *The Wall Street Journal*, today it's the Internet. And if they're priced right, they sell. Acquisitions are always a challenge, especially if you're going into a new market. That's the most fun for me.

You make the money on the acquisition, and – I'll usually, if it's a place I'm not familiar with, I'll send the acquisition department out there. But I'm always out there, knocking on doors and visiting comps and going in and playing tenant and being in the building I'm going to buy, and then when I show up 30 days later for the walk-through, the lady says, "I remember you." It's fun, and it's simple to do because I do the same thing. Some people ask me, "Why don't you do some other kind of real estate?" I would say, "Because I don't know it. I don't understand it. But I understand apartments."

**That's like Warren Buffett, just do what you know how to do. There's plenty there. You're doing what you know how to do and you're great at doing it.**

And it's the same thing with new markets. I mean, we're in six markets now and if you can't find good deals in those six markets – they're all major markets – then something's wrong with you, not the business or the market.

**What are you doing to position your company to take advantage of today's great buying opportunity?**

We started the Opportunity Fund a little over a year ago. Our business used to be, for the past twelve or fourteen years, tenant-in-common driven which was probably 80 or 90% of our fundraising and that has kind of gone away because the tenant-in-common doesn't want to sell his property at what he perceives to be a loss, so the Opportunity Fund is really designed not to accept any tenant-in-common. So it's a little bit of a start-up for us because our traditional source for raising funds is not really there. And a lot of the registered reps who sold for us were just totally focused on tenant-in-common, and so their book, if you will, went away. So we're having to start back up, and we're probably only raising about a third of what we used to raise, but I think that will continue to grow.

**Where are you going to raise your money?**

Broker-dealers. We have our direct investor's who have been with us forever, and they're always there. But for growth, it's broker-dealers. We have selling agreements with probably 25 different broker-dealers and access to tens of thousands of representatives. And it's just a matter of reaching out to these guys and making them familiar with what we do. A lot of them want a certain percentage of their clients' money invested in real estate, and some of them like the more local approach as opposed to a big REIT, and it's more individualized. The Opportunity Fund only has two buildings in it, and we may close it with only those two and start the next fund.

**How are you sourcing deals?**

Pretty much the Internet. I'd say we are on everybody's database and everyone is on ours. We see everything that's out there. We certainly have tried to work directly with lenders, and it's my impression that we're doing it right, but it's not like last time.

**You bought a couple of properties in Florida that you turned around and added value to. Could you give us an example of that?**

One was a failed condo conversion called Wilton Manor in Fort Lauderdale, and it was a foreclosure with B of A. It's an example, kind of what I was talking about. We have a relationship with B of A where we are a pretty big depositor with them. We tracked this building before they filed notice of default. I actually went by it because it's not too far from my home in Fort Lauderdale, and I saw this 11-story building with no cars in the parking lot. And it wasn't brand new; it was older, and so something's going on here.

I had acquisitions research it, and they found out that it was a condo conversion in the offering, and they were clearly failing, and then we contacted B of A, and they said, "Well, we're working with the borrower," and ended up filing a notice of default and putting a receiver in. This whole process took 18 months, and we offered to buy the building from them from the beginning, but they had to go through the process. We ended up being one of eleven bidders and I think because we had known of this building for so long, we knew it better than anyone else, and I was willing to go hard with a bigger deposit, we got the building. It is only 150 units, but I put about $2.2 million into it – new kitchens, bathrooms, granite, new cabinets, resort-style pool, new gym, new business center, and just made it gorgeous. I raised the rents about 30%. It's been a little over a year, and we just hit 93% occupancy.

**It took you about a year to get stabilized?**

Yes, because the building was built in the middle '70s, and so the original kitchens were horrible. When we closed escrow, it had been run by the receiver and it had like 50 units vacant. But I wasn't about to rent any of those in their current condition. So we had to go get permits, order all the material, and probably didn't have the first units rehabbed for maybe 120 days after the close of escrow.

So it's been a matter of going through that, where as the other building, Windward Village, in Palm Beach was 95% occupied when we closed it. It was a newer building, and it was owned by a REIT, and they had redone about eight units, similar to what I had done at Wilton and they had been able to raise the rents $100.00. So I budgeted to do the same thing in Palm Beach, but not empty the building, and just kind of do them as they became vacant. And so we have been able to do that and aintain our occupancy in the mid-90s.

**What do you look for in a great deal?**

I would say location is probably the number one thing that I look for. I don't really want to do C properties. I've had C properties, and they're just too labor intensive and the tenants can destroy everything. For me, they don't work. The ideal would be a property with good bones that has deferred maintenance, but has potential sitting in an A area with brand new buildings all around it. We can go in and be 15% below them on rents, but give them a similar product. That would be an ideal situation.

**Talk to us about your property management. I know that's one of the cornerstones of your success – aggressive property management.**

It is, and I think it's because when I first started in the middle '70s, I did it myself, and when I left my job with Victor, I didn't have any income, I just had these little apartment buildings. So I'm out there doing everything, and I basically learned how to make it all it could be, and I'm very involved in property management here.

My director of property management has been with me around 23 years and the head of maintenance, 25 or 26 years. So you know, I can still go out and look at a building and basically tell you what's wrong with it. If we're not renting, it's usually the staff. You can go in and determine that pretty quickly, and if there's something little that you can do to improve the curb appeal. I can see that, and I think that's the fact that I am involved. You'll meet a lot of people in our business that they never go out and visit the properties, and I still visit every property probably three times a year.

## Who are some of your business and personal heroes that you've had throughout your career?

I think Warren Buffett's a good example. Sam Zell is too. He's maybe made some mistakes recently, but I think anyone who does it right realizes that real estate is a get-rich-slow business, not a get-rich-fast business, and safety is the most important thing, and being fair to all involved.

### Willam "Rance" King, Jr
Founder, RK Properties

RK Properties was founded in 1976 by William "Rance" King, Jr. (RK) after a ten year history in business machines for a Fortune 500 company. He was a pioneer in developing and marketing early style computers that were sold to a variety of industries, primarily focused on commercial real estate. By the time he became National Director of Sales, he had already purchased his first apartment building, which was the inception of what would become RK Properties.

In the beginning, RK Properties did Tenant-in-Common (TIC) deals with a small group of business associates and friends. This eventually evolved into the limited partnership business, then into Limited Liability Corporations until, in the 1990's, the TIC structure dominated the real estate market. Over the past 34 years, RK Properties has syndicated 156 properties and had 126 properties go full cycle, a 'track record' of success that simply does not exist with any other firm.

# *About the Author*
## *Craig Haskell*

Craig Haskell is founder of *Haskell Value Real Estate Investor*, the only online publication dedicated exclusively to opportunistic and value minded real estate investors. Craig is also founder of Value Hound Academy, a leading training and coaching platform for new and experienced real estate value investors on how to make more money with their investments.

Craig's unique understanding of value real estate investing is reinventing the way value investors do business to achieve high risk adjusted returns. As an inspiring leader and in-demand speaker, trainer and coach, Craig has helped hundreds of investors and organizations around the world to become more successful value real estate investors.

Craig has interviewed some of today's leading and smartest value minded real estate investors such as Gary Sabin CEO of Excel Trust, Michael Brennan Co-Founder of Brennan Investment Group, Jerry Fink Co-Founder of The Bascom Group, Michael Schwartz CEO of Strategic Storage Trust, Ryan Krauch Principal of Mesa West Capital, and many more.

Craig has devoted over 25 years to value real estate investing, and has owned and managed 7,200 units and 2.8 million square feet of commercial space and provided advisory services on over $2 billion. Craig is also author of *How to Take an Apartment Building from Money Pit to Money Maker, Secrets of Successful Apartment Buildings* and *A Guide to Creating Successful Apartment Advertisements*.

As the creator of the Value Hound Blueprint, a value investing system for real estate value investors, Craig is the nation's leading expert on the subject of value real estate investing. Meet Craig at www.HaskellValueRealEstateInvestor.com

Made in the USA
Lexington, KY
27 August 2013